Crossway Bible Guide

Series editors: Ian Coffey (NT), Stephen Gaukroger (OT)
New Testament editor: Stephen Motyer

Also in this series:

Exodus: Stephen Dray
Leviticus: Derek Tidball
Joshua: Charles Price
Ezra and Nehemiah: Dave Cave
Psalms 1–72: Alan Palmer
Isaiah: Philip Hacking
Six minor prophets: Michael Wilcock
Haggai, Zechariah and Malachi: John James
Mark's gospel: David Hewitt
John's gospel: Ian Barclay
Acts: Stephen Gaukroger
1 Corinthians: Robin Dowling and Stephen Dray
Ephesians: Stephen Motyer
Philippians: Ian Coffey
Timothy and Titus: Michael Griffiths
James: David Field
1 Peter: Andrew Whitman

The Bible with pleasure: Stephen Motyer
Housegroups: the leaders' survival guide: Ian Coffey and Stephen Gaukroger

Dedication

This book is dedicated to the fellowship which meets at New Cross Road Baptist Church, London SE14. It was they who first encouraged me to write and gave me time to do so. It was they, too, who shared with me for a number of years a common pilgrimage through the gospel of Matthew.

Matthew's gospel: Crossway Bible Guide

Stephen Dray

Crossway Books Leicester

CROSSWAY BOOKS
38 De Montfort Street, Leicester LE1 7GP, England

First published 1998

British Library Cataloguing in Publication Data
A catalogue record for this book is available from the British Library.

ISBN 1–85684–175–8

Set in Palatino

Typeset in Great Britain by Textype Typesetters, Cambridge
Printed in Great Britain by The Guernsey Press Co. Ltd., Guernsey, Channel Islands

CONTENTS

Welcome!

These days, meeting together to study the Bible in groups appears to be a booming leisure-time activity in many parts of the world. In the United Kingdom alone, it is estimated that over one million people each week meet in home Bible-study groups.

This series has been designed to help such groups and, in particular, those who lead them, but it is also very suitable for individual study. We are aware of the needs of those who preach and teach larger groups as well as the hard-pressed student, all of whom often look for a commentary that gives a concise summary and lively application of a particular passage.

We have therefore enlisted authors who are in the business of teaching the Bible to others and are doing it well. They have kept in their sights two clear aims:

1. To explain and apply the message of the Bible in non-technical language.
2. To encourage discussion, prayer and action on what the Bible teaches.

All of us engaged in the project believe that the Bible is the Word of God – given to us in order that people might discover him and his purposes for our lives. We believe that the sixty-six books which go to make up the Bible, although written by different people, in different places, at different times, through different circumstances, have a single unifying theme: that theme is Salvation. This means free forgiveness and the removal of all our guilt, it means the gift of eternal life, and it means the wholeness of purpose and joy which God has designed us to experience here and now, all of this being made possible through the Lord Jesus Christ.

How to use this Bible Guide

These guides have been prepared both for personal study and for the leaders and members of small groups. More information about group study follows on the next few pages.

You can use this book very profitably as a personal study guide. The short studies are ideal for daily reading: the first of the questions provided is usually aimed to help you with personal reflection (see *How to tackle personal Bible study*). If you prefer to settle down to a longer period of study, you can use groups of three to five studies, and thus get a better overview of a longer Bible passage. In either case, using the Bible Guide will help you to be disciplined about regular study, a habit that countless Christians have found greatly beneficial. (See also *How to tackle Matthew* for methods of selecting studies if you do not intend to use them all.)

Yet a third use for these Bible Guides is as a quarry for ideas for the busy Bible teacher, providing outlines and application for those giving talks or sermons or teaching children. You will need more than this book can offer, of course, but the way the Bible text is broken down, comments offered and questions raised, may well suggest directions to follow.

How to tackle personal Bible study

We have already suggested that you might use this book as a personal study guide. Now for some more detail.

One of the best methods of Bible study is to read the text through carefully several times, possibly using different versions or translations. Having reflected on the material, it is a good discipline to write down your own thoughts before doing anything else. At this stage it can be useful to refer to another background book. See *Resources* on page 13 and *Further reading* on page 245. If you are using this book as your main study resource, then read through the relevant sections carefully, turning up the Bible references that are mentioned. The questions at the end of each chapter are specifically designed to help you to apply the passage to your own situtation. You may find it helpful to write your answers to the questions in your notes.

It is a good habit to conclude with prayer, bringing before God the things you have learned.

If this kind of in-depth study is too demanding for you and you have only a short time at your disposal, read the Bible passage, read the comments in the Bible Guide, think round one of the questions and commit what you have learned to God in a brief prayer. This would take about fifteen minutes without rushing it.

How to tackle your group Bible study

1. Getting help

If you are new to leading groups, you will obviously want to get all the help you can from ministers and experienced friends. Books are also extremely helpful and we strongly recommend a book prepared by the editors of this series of Bible Guides: *Housegroups: the leaders' survival guide,* edited by Ian Coffey and Stephen Gaukroger (Crossway Books, 1996). This book looks at the whole range of different types of group, asking what is the point of it all, what makes a good leader, how to tackle your meeting, how to help the members, how to study, pray, share, worship and plenty of other pointers, tips and guidelines.

This book is a 'must' for all leaders of small groups. It is written by a team of people widely experienced in this area. It is available at your local Christian bookshop. If you have difficulty in obtaining a copy write to Crossway Books, Norton Street, Nottingham, NG7 3HR, UK.

2. Planning a programme with your Bible Guide

This guide is a commentary on God's Word, written to help a group to get the most out of their studies. Although it is never ideal to chop up Scripture into small pieces, which the authors never intended, huge chunks are indigestible and we have tried to provide a diet of bite-sized mouthfuls.

If you want to get an overview of the Bible book in a series of meetings, you will need to select appropriate studies for each meeting. Read them yourself first and prepare a short summary of the studies you are tackling for your group. Ideally you could write it on a sheet of A5 paper and hand a copy to each member.

Do not attempt to pack more than one study into one meeting but choose the crucial one, the study which best crystallizes the message. There are examples in *How to tackle Matthew's gospel* below.

If you do not intend to cover the whole Bible book, choose a series of studies to suit the number of meetings you have available. It is a good idea to use consecutive studies, not to dodge about. You will then build up a detailed picture of one section of Scripture. Alternative examples of programmes of study for this book are given in *How to tackle Matthew's gospel*.

3. Resources

You will find any or all of these books of great value in providing background to your Bible knowledge. Put some of them on your Christmas list and build up your library.

New Bible Dictionary or *New Concise Bible Dictionary* (IVP)
New Bible Atlas (IVP)
New Bible Commentary (21st Century edition) (IVP)
Handbook of Life in Bible Times: John Thompson (IVP)
The Bible User's Manual (IVP)
The Lion Handbook to the Bible (Lion Publishing)
The Message of the Bible (Lion Publishing)
NIV Study Bible (Hodder & Stoughton)
The Bible with Pleasure: Stephen Motyer (Crossway Books)

The relevant volume in the IVP Tyndale Commentary series will give you reliable and detailed help with any knotty points you may encounter.

4. Preparing to lead

Reading, discussing with friends, studying, praying, reflecting on life . . . preparation can be endless. But do not be daunted by that. If you wait to become the perfect leader you will never start at all. The really vital elements in preparation are:

- prayer (not only words but an attitude of dependence on God: 'Lord, I can't manage this on my own');
- familiarity with the study passage (careful reading of the text, the Bible Guide study and any other resource books that throw light on it); and
- a clear idea of where you hope to get in the meeting (notes on your introduction, perhaps, recap what was covered at the last meeting, and what direction you hope the questions will take you in – don't force the group to give your answers).

Here is a short checklist for the busy group leader:

Have I prayed about the meeting?
Have I decided exactly what I want to achieve through the meeting?
Have I prepared the material?
Am I clear about the questions that will encourage positive group discussion?
Am I gently encouraging silent members?
Am I, again gently, quietening the chatterers?
Am I willing to admit ignorance?
Am I willing to listen to what the group says and to value their contributions?
Am I ready not to be dogmatic, not imposing my ideas on the group?
Have I planned how to involve the group in discovering for themselves?
Have I developed several 'prayer points' that will help focus the group?
Are we applying Scripture to our experience of real life or only using it as a peg to hang our opinions on?
Are we finding resources for action and change or just having a nice talk?
Are we all enjoying the experience together?

How to tackle *Matthew's gospel*

Now let's assume you are planning an eight-week course of studies (you will have to make the adjustments if you have more or fewer meetings). Where do you begin? This is entirely up to you and your group of course but, to get you started, here are a few possible routes you might take.

1. A bird's-eye view of the gospel

God becomes human for us (1:18–25)
Put to the test (4:1–11)
Right attitudes (5:1–6)
Anxiety and how to avoid it (6:25–34)
The Messiah gives a banquet and walks on water (14:13–36)
Waiting for Jesus' return (24:1–14)
Jesus' death (27:27–56)
Facing the evidence (27:57 – 28:15)

2. Studies in the Sermon on the Mount

Right attitudes (5:1–6)
Watch out! Persecution's about! (5:10–12)
Salt and light (5:13–16)
Adultery and divorce (5:27–32)*
True prayer (6:5–15)
Anxiety and how to avoid it (6:25–34)
Criticize with care! (7:1–12)
Watch out for 'jerry building'! (7:24–29)

* Your group may well contain divorced people. If so (and this is too sensitive an issue to deal with in public), choose another passage, for example 'Swearing and going the second mile' (5:33–42).

3. A selection of parables

Listening to Jesus (the sower) (13:1–11)
Side by side (the weeds) (13:24–30, 36–43)
Caring and forgiveness (the unmerciful servant) (18:15–35)
God's sovereign grace (the workers in the vineyard) (20:1–19)
A message for all nations (the wedding banquet) (22:1–14)
Coming again. Be prepared! (the ten virgins) (24:36 – 25:13)

Called to faithful service (the talents) (25:14–30)
Serving at the kitchen sink (the sheep and the goats) (25:31–46)

4. The story of the passion

The last eight studies cover chapters 26 to 28, and these would make an excellent series leading up to Easter.

These outlines are meant to be springboards for your own ideas, so please do not follow them slavishly. Adapt them for your own use, merge them or ignore them. In any case much of Matthew will go unread if you concentrate only on these short snippets. You as leader will need to read carefully the whole book so that you can refer your group to sections they have not read. It would be wise to read a whole chapter when studying a part of it – the context often throws light on the verses you are looking at.

What can we expect to learn from *Matthew's gospel*?

- Jesus is the fulfilment of all the hopes and expectations of the Old Testament.
- Jesus is the Messiah and God-made-man. He shows this by the authority of his teaching and the nature of his miracles.
- The stories about Jesus are historical fact. Matthew was recording the truth.
- Jesus' teaching, particularly about the kingdom of God, what is expected of Christians, and specific matters like remarriage and divorce.
- Jesus is the hope of the world. Matthew shows how the Good News applies to everyone.

Finding your way round this book

In our Bible Guides we have developed special symbols to make things easier to follow. Every study therefore has an opening section which is the passage in a nutshell.

The main section is the one that *makes sense of the passage.*

Questions

Every passage also has special questions for personal and group study after the main section. Some questions are addressed to us as individuals, some speak to us as members of our church or home group, while others concern us as members of God's people worldwide. The questions are deliberately designed:

- to get people thinking about the passage
- to apply the text to 'real life' situations
- to encourage reflection, discussion and action

As a group leader you may well discover additional questions that will have special relevance to your group, so look out for these and note them in your preparation time.

Digging deeper

Some passages, however, require an extra amount of explanation, and we have put these sections into two categories. The first kind gives additional background material that helps us to understand something factual. For example, if we dig deeper into the gospels, it helps us to know who the Pharisees were, so that we can see more easily why they related to Jesus in the way they did. These technical sections are marked with a spade.

Important doctrines

The second kind of background section appears with passages which have important doctrines contained in them and which we need to study in more depth if we are to grow as Christians. Special sections that explain them to us in greater detail are marked with a face as above.

Introducing *Matthew's gospel*

Who wrote 'the gospel of Matthew'?

The gospel of Matthew is anonymous. There is nothing within it to identify the author. However, the earliest traditions of the church all agree that the gospel was written by the disciple of Jesus named in Matthew 9:9. The content of the gospel is what we might have expected Matthew/Levi to write as a Jew, a respecter of authority, and a man totally convinced of the kingship of Jesus Christ. The tradition is therefore probably correct. It is assumed in this book.

When was the gospel written?

Again, nothing is said within the gospel about the date when it was written. Traditionally it was regarded as the original one of the four gospels (hence its place at the beginning of the New Testament). During the last century, however, opinion has swung towards Mark being viewed as the first gospel, and Matthew is regarded as dependent on Mark and on supplementary material available to him alone. Since Mark has often been dated to the seventh decade of the Christian era, Matthew has usually been dated to the AD 70s.

Today, nothing is so certain! These traditional arguments are increasingly under attack. Existing early copies of parts of the New Testament are being dated ever earlier, and there are those who think that Matthew would have included references to the fall of Jerusalem (AD 70) if he had written his gospel after the event. It is far from unlikely that the gospel of Matthew was written as early as the mid 40s or soon afterwards. If this is the case, it would have been written very soon after the events described, within recent memory both of the author and those who read this story. All this tends to confirm the historical reliability of what is recounted.

Why was the gospel written?

A careful study of the gospel of Matthew suggests that it was probably written to Jews to convince its readers that Jesus was the promised Messiah. The appeal to Jesus' genealogy, the claims that the events associated with Jesus' birth fulfilled Old Testament messianic Scriptures, the interest in the law and other 'Jewish' customs (see 15:1–9), etc., all suggest that the gospel was written with Jews especially in mind. It is true that Matthew insists that the gospel is relevant to all nations (see, especially, 28:16–20). However, even in this, Matthew is surely drawing attention to the fundamental calling of the people of God in the Old Testament (compare Genesis 12:1–3).

Thus, there appears to be no good reason to doubt the usual claim that Matthew was written to Jews as a sort of evangelistic booklet.

Matthew 1:1–17

It's true! God saves

The stories about Jesus in the gospels really happened. They tell us how God completed his plans to save men and women from their sins.

The first book in the New Testament was written by Matthew, a tax collector who became one of Jesus' closest friends and followers. (See Matthew 9:9–13; and also Mark 2:13–17; Luke 5:27–32.)

Matthew wanted his readers to understand that what he was writing down actually happened. The first words of his book are often translated 'This is the genealogy of . . .', as though he was just introducing verses 2–17. But his words are probably best understood as introducing the whole book and saying, 'This is the history book of Jesus Christ'. Many of us are so used to using Jesus Christ as a name that we miss the fact that 'Christ' was originally a title. The word means 'anointed one' and was used by the Jews to describe the great deliverer that God had promised in the Old Testament Scriptures. The Jews of Matthew's time hoped that the 'Christ' would deliver them from the power of the Romans who had occupied their land for many years.

'Jesus' means 'he will certainly save' (see verse 21). The Jews expected the Christ to have the name of Jesus, so many mothers, hoping that their child would be the Christ, gave their sons this name. Matthew believed that this Jesus – the son of Joseph and

Mary – was the Christ. However, Jesus came to bring about a far greater deliverance than the Jews ever imagined: he would conquer sin (verse 21) and establish a kingdom far greater than the wildest dreams of the Jews!

Two of the Old Testament passages which spoke of the coming Christ were Genesis 22:18 and 2 Samuel 7:12–16. Because of these prophecies, the Jews believed that the coming deliverer would be a descendant of both Abraham and David, the two greatest 'Jews' who had ever lived. Matthew tells us that Jesus met this condition, for he was 'the son of David, the son of Abraham'.

Roots!

Today there is an increasing interest in tracing one's ancestors. In many parts of the world such knowledge has always been of vital importance. This was true among the Jews, and careful records were kept either in the memories of the oldest members or in writing. Since Matthew was writing especially to Jews, it was important that he should give the proof to support the claims he had already made.

This list at the beginning of Matthew is divided into three sections, each containing fourteen names (verses 2–6a, 6b–11, 12–17). The first section begins with Abraham, who was the first man to receive the promise that the great deliverer would be one of his descendants (Genesis 12:1–3). It ends with David, Israel's greatest king. In this way Matthew traced out God's promise upon an entirely human level. Until the time when Matthew lived, David had been the greatest-ever descendant of Abraham. However, after David died, his kingdom was split into two parts and the glory of his kingdom faded. Yet greater promises had been given to him than to Abraham (2 Samuel 7). Who was the promised deliverer who would be greater even than David?

In the second part of the list, Matthew traces the descendants of David up to the exile. Even by Matthew's day there had been no credible claimant to be God's promised one. At least, this was true until Jesus came. Matthew will show that Jesus did indeed fulfil all the hopes expressed in the Old Testament promises!

Questions

1. How would you respond to those who say it is the religious 'truth' that the stories about Jesus contain that is important, not whether or not they ever really happened?
2. What does your church fellowship think is the most important thing to tell non-Christians? Do you agree with Matthew's own emphasis, that 'God saves'?
3. Is your Christianity one that focuses upon the kingdom that Jesus will one day establish, or are you more concerned for what you can get from him now? Share your ideas with the group.
4. Consider God's promises to Abraham in Genesis 12:1–3 and to David in 1 Samuel 7. How do you think they are fulfilled in Jesus?

Matthew 1:18–25

God becomes human for us

Jesus was God. He was also fully human. The story of his birth shows how this can be true.

Matthew has told us that Jesus is the promised Christ and has shown us that Jesus had the right credentials. We are on tiptoe waiting for the story to begin! He does not tell us everything that was known about Jesus' birth but we are told enough to be sure of two great facts: first, that Jesus was born of a virgin and, second, Jesus' strange birth has very special significance.

During the betrothal year of Jesus' parents (see Jewish Marriage Customs, p. 25), Joseph discovered that Mary was pregnant. His response was natural: he assumed that Mary had been unfaithful to him. God's law demanded action and Joseph sought to honour God in his life. However, he did not act on impulse. While still thinking about what to do, Joseph had a vivid dream which he knew was from God. An angel brought the most unbelievable message to Joseph. Although she was pregnant, Mary had not been unfaithful to him and she was still a virgin! Her child was God's in a unique way, because the Holy Spirit had made her pregnant. Joseph was reminded that this is exactly what God had predicted would happen when the Christ was born. As a man familiar with the Old Testament Scriptures, the words from Isaiah 7:14 would have been well known to him.

Joseph's reaction was heroic. He obeyed God's messenger and married Mary. Doubtless he heard many a snigger behind his back from those who assumed he had had pre-marital sex with Mary. Some of his friends, perhaps knowing him better, would have criticized him for disobeying the law of God. He might sometimes have heard his wife described as a whore. Obeying God is not always easy!

Matthew explains why this strange event took place. God became a man to 'save his people from their sins' (verse 21). The whole of the Old Testament (as well as the whole of human history) shows that men and women, though capable of many good and worthwhile acts, are flawed by sin. As such, they are unable to help themselves and they need to be rescued from their sad condition. However, more than that, the Bible teaches plainly that sinful people have set themselves against God and must, eventually, be punished by him. With these verses Matthew begins to hint at a truth which he will explain more fully in the pages to come.

Questions

1. Is there any area of your life where, like Joseph, you are being called by God to heroic action? What might you learn from this passage to encourage you to be faithful and persevering?
2. The Virgin Birth is only mentioned clearly twice in the New Testament. Why do you think that it is important for

Christians to believe and teach it?

3. We live in a world that is often full of pain and sorrow. What message does this passage give your church to proclaim and to do for a sad and hurting world?

Jewish marriage customs

There were three stages to a Jewish marriage. First, there was the engagement, which was often made when the couple were still children since, as in many places today, marriage was often arranged through a 'marriage-broker' by the parents. This could happen without the couple having seen one another, and marriage was regarded as far too serious a matter to leave to the emotional whims of young people. The second stage in the 'marriage' was the betrothal. This was a formal agreement between the two young people that the engagement should stand. At this point an engagement could be broken off if the girl was unwilling to go through with it. However, once the betrothal took place it was absolutely binding. It lasted one year, and during this time the couple were addressed as man and wife, although they did not live together. Termination could only take place during this period by divorce. This is the stage that Mary and Joseph had reached when we are first introduced to them. At the end of the betrothal year the marriage took place.

Joseph is described as a 'righteous man'. This means that he was faithful to the laws which God had given to Israel. According to those laws, a promiscuous woman was to be divorced after a public trial (Deuteronomy 22:23ff.). By the time of Joseph and Mary, the death penalty by stoning had ceased. However, there was another way to deal with the 'problem'. Deuteronomy 24:1–2 was believed to justify a 'secret' divorce. Since Joseph was a kind man, he decided upon this second course of action. In this way Mary's shame would be minimized.

Virgin birth

Matthew's picture of the 'virgin birth' of Jesus has often been challenged even by theologians.

Some Old Testament scholars have questioned Matthew's quotation of Isaiah 7:14 in verse 23. Although Matthew writes 'virgin', they argue that Isaiah used a word that simply means 'young woman' (Hebrew, *'almâ*). However, *'almâ* is in fact the nearest word to 'virgin' in Hebrew, and while it does not absolutely exclude the possibility of sexual relations having taken place, it hints at virginity, since it is derived from a word meaning 'secret, hidden or sealed up'. It is also yet to be proved that it is ever used of a married person in the Old Testament. The alternative explanation would seem to be that, even if Isaiah did refer to the immediate future, both the Greek translators and Matthew might have seen that Isaiah's prophecy pointed, by way of illustration, to a still more remarkable sign, in which the word *'almâ* would have its fullest force. Either way, we have no reason to believe that the Bible is in error or that the New Testament writers took liberties with the meaning of the Old Testament Scriptures.

Matthew 2:1–12

A royal priest

The visit of the wise men ('Magi') shows that Jesus is a king, a priest and God himself. It also suggests that his life of obedience to God will bring him great suffering.

Matthew does not give us the story of Jesus' birth. His main interest is in explaining its significance, by describing some strange events that took place some time later.

Jesus was born exactly as the Old Testament Scriptures had predicted. The prophet Micah, who had lived over 800 years earlier, had promised that after the exile a great ruler would once again be born in Lesser Bethlehem, the place where David had been born (Micah 5:2). No-one had ever arisen to fulfil the promise, and the Jewish people were still waiting (verses 4–5). But Jesus was born in the small village from which Micah had predicted the great deliverer would come!

The fact that Matthew records the gifts that the Magi brought to Jesus suggests that he believed they each tell us something particular:

- Even today *gold* often symbolizes royalty; but in the Old Testament it was also a sign of holiness, used extensively in the decoration of the temple (1 Kings 6:20–22).
- *Frankincense* was a perfume much used in ancient times and, among the Jews, it was especially used by the priests in the temple. In the Old Testament, one of the chief duties of the priests was to make offerings, usually of perfect animals. These offerings were seen as 'substitutionary', for the animals were actually dying in the place of the person who brought the offering. They were also regarded as 'penal', which means that the offering was seen as a price

being paid to God as the penalty for having failed him.

- *Myrrh* was another perfume, which was used in Bible times to relieve pain and to make burial less horrible. It had also been used in the Old Testament to symbolize faithfulness to God.

Matthew seems to have believed that these gifts symbolized the fact that Jesus was a holy king, obedient to God, in whose priestly service he would suffer and die.

Matthew may also have wanted us to reflect on the different reactions that people had to the news of Jesus' birth. Herod (see p. 29) knew and believed God's word and he had no doubts that the Magi would find the Christ in Bethlehem, for he said to them, 'when you find him' (verse 8). But Herod was more interested in himself and his own ambitions. So he tried to defeat God!

If Herod was led astray by worldly ambition, the chief priests and teachers of the law (see p. 30) had a different problem: they were professional Bible experts who simply failed to apply God's word to themselves. They showed very little interest in the news of the Magi. The whole of the Old Testament points forward to Jesus, and yet these men seemed uninterested in the very one to whom all their studies pointed.

The Magi had little knowledge of Jesus, but they travelled great distances and overcame some enormous difficulties in order to find him. And when they first saw him, even though he was only a tiny baby in the arms of his mother, they honoured him. Indeed, these men 'worshipped' Jesus. Worship is never offered in the New Testament (at least, not without being rebuked) except to God. Matthew tells us that the baby in the arms of Mary was God himself and, in some way, even the Magi knew this!

Questions

1. What lessons can be learned from the different reactions of people to Jesus in this passage?

2. Jesus came into this world to live in obedience to his Father and to serve us – even to the point of death. What implications does that have for our church life?
3. What does this passage teach us about the content of the gospel which we are called to share with others?

Herod

There are several different Herods mentioned in the Bible. Herod the Great ruled Palestine at the time of Jesus' birth. He was born in 73 BC and was king from 40 BC until 4 BC. He was a murderous man and lived with the fear that he would be assassinated. At the time of his death he was planning to kill over 3,000 people, and earlier he had killed his wife, brother-in-law, mother and some of his sons because he feared them. All this explains his reaction to the report of the Magi. It also helps us to understand why 'all Jerusalem' was also troubled – when Herod got worried, others normally suffered! Shortly, the mothers of Bethlehem would experience the king's cruelty.

It is possible that Herod was especially worried because the Magi spoke of someone 'born king of the Jews'. Herod himself had gained the kingship by intrigue.

Jesus was born a short time before Herod's death (compare verses 1 and 19). Herod died shortly after an eclipse of the moon at the end of March or the beginning of April in 4 BC. Jesus was probably born in 5 BC.

The Magi and the star

Magi were the religious leaders and wise men in Persia and Media (now Iran and the surrounding countries). We are not told how they came to their knowledge about Jesus. Perhaps it was by a dream similar to that described in verse 12. The view that a great deliverer would arise among the Jews may have influenced them.

Many attempts have been made to identify the star which the Magi saw. Halley's Comet is often suggested as likely, but this appeared in 12 BC, too early to have marked out Jesus' birth. A more likely contender is a comet recorded by Chinese astronomers, which appeared in 5 BC and would have behaved in the unusual way described in verses 9 and 10. Its tail would have pointed downward 'over' Bethlehem. (For details, see *Tyndale Bulletin* 43.1, 1992.)

The chief priests and the teachers of the law

These men were the ruling religious and political leaders in ancient Judea. They met together in a gathering called the Sanhedrin. The chief priests included the ruling High Priest, those who had formerly held the office, and the group from whom the High Priest was usually chosen. They were all members of the Sadducees (see p. 39). The teachers of the law (often called 'scribes' in some English translations of the Bible) were responsible for upholding the laws of God and teaching God's words. They were the experts in Jewish religion and were usually Pharisees (see p. 39).

Matthew 2:13–23

God is in charge

God keeps his promises and he protects and cares for his children.

In three short paragraphs (verses 13–15, 16–18, 19–23) Matthew completes his account of the early life of Jesus.

Herod reacted promptly and typically when he realized that the Magi were not coming back. Probably only a few days had passed since the visit of the Magi and Jesus was only weeks old. However, Herod makes absolutely sure that there will be no rival king by killing all the children under the age of two. Although Bethlehem was only a very small village, it is probable that between fifteen and thirty helpless children were slaughtered by Herod.

However, human beings cannot stop God's plans. Herod himself was the one who was shortly to die, and Jesus was able to escape the murderous plot anyway! God told Joseph of the danger in advance, and he was able to take the child and Mary away to the nearest safe place: to Egypt.

Verses 19–23 describe the return of Joseph's family to Israel after Herod's death. We are not surprised that Joseph was unwilling to return to Bethlehem since the new ruler, Archelaus, was as bad as his father and had already had 3,000 people put to death. God understood Joseph's anxiety and encouraged Joseph to return to his former home in Nazareth (see Luke 2:4), which was not in Archelaus's territory. So God was keeping and caring for Jesus and his family, despite all the dangers. He will do the same for us.

Jesus fulfils God's promises in the Old Testament. Each of the three short paragraphs conclude with quotations from the Old Testament which, Matthew tells us, Jesus fulfilled (see Matthew's use of the Old Testament, pp. 32–34).

Finally, we note that Joseph was obedient to God but did not always find it easy. His life was disrupted by Mary's pregnancy and the birth of Jesus. Sometimes he was bewildered and anxious, not knowing which way to turn, only knowing that the Lord had brought him so far. On other occasions he knew part of God's plan but not all of it (compare verses 20 and 22). We have already seen the criticism he doubtless attracted by marrying Mary (p. 24). Despite all this, Joseph learned that obedience was the best way, for God kept him, even in the midst of great danger.

Questions

1. Reflect upon the experience of Joseph and apply the lessons of his life to yourself in your present circumstances.
2. What encouragement does this passage offer your fellowship? How does God's guidance come to you as a body of believers?
3. Reflecting on the massacre recorded in 2:16, write a letter to your local newspaper showing how the message of Christmas speaks to a suffering world.

Matthew's use of the Old Testament

How do these Old Testament passages apply to Jesus? At first reading in the Old Testament they do not seem to have anything to do with him!

Verse 15 is a quotation from Hosea 11:1. In that passage the prophet spoke of God's deliverance of the Israelites from Egypt many hundreds of years earlier. How then can the passage apply to Jesus? Did Matthew misuse the Scriptures or use them in a way customary among the Jews but unacceptable today? A careful study of the way the New Testament writers used the Old shows that they saw parallels between the Old Testament story and Jesus' life and work. They felt that, in a strange way, Jesus fulfilled the whole history of Israel and even re-enacted it. Israel had been called out of Egypt to bring God's salvation to the world. She failed. However, where she failed, Jesus would succeed. Thus, he, too, went down into Egypt and returned, in order to demonstrate that he had come to save the world and bring the knowledge of God to all mankind. Hosea was not predicting this, of course, but his words could be used quite fairly to make Matthew's point.

In verse 18 Matthew is making a similar point. He quotes Jeremiah 31:15, a passage which predicted the sorrow in Bethlehem when the young people of the village would be led away into the exile. As such, the words could not refer directly to Herod's murder of the babies. However, Jeremiah's words were a message of hope, for the surrounding verses of his prophecy declared that, though the land should suffer the devastation of war and exile, hope and deliverance would certainly follow, for God had not forgotten his people nor the promises he had made to them. Once again Matthew saw a parallel between those days and his own. For just as God had once brought hope and deliverance to a sad people so, in Jesus, he had done it again. Jesus brings hope to desperate people, the hope that the world had long sought for, deliverance from sin.

Verse 23 is a little more difficult, because Matthew does not tell us where the Scripture is to be found. Some have suggested that he is thinking of Isaiah 11:1 where the word 'branch' is used: a word which sounds in Hebrew like 'Nazareth'. Others think that Numbers 6 is in mind, because of its mention of the 'Nazirite'. It is certainly true that Jesus fulfils both of these passages. However, these words only sound similar to the name Nazareth: they have no real connection with it. Since Matthew actually quotes 'the prophets', it is, in fact, more likely that he had a number of scriptures in mind. In fact, Nazareth was a despised village (see John 1:45–46), and Matthew knew that time and again in the Old Testament it was predicted that the Christ would be despised. So, for instance, Psalms 22:6–8, 13; 69:8, 20–21; Isaiah 11:1; 49:7; 53:2–3, 8; and Daniel 9:26 either describe the righteous as being despised, or look forward to the Messiah who will, above all, be the despised yet righteous one.

Matthew and the other New Testament writers realized such language applied especially to Jesus (compare 12:24; 27:21–23, 63; Luke 23:11; John 1:11; 5:18; 6:66; 9:22, 34).

Matthew 3:1–3

Be ready!

Only those who are truly repentant will enjoy the benefits of Jesus' ministry.

Abruptly, Matthew moves on to describe several events which took place thirty years later and immediately before Jesus began his public ministry. He clearly regarded what happened as very significant because his first phrase, 'in those days', really means, 'in those important, crucial days'.

Great leaders usually send a messenger or herald in advance to enable full preparations to be made for them. Jesus was a king (2:2). He also had a herald, one who (and we are getting used to Matthew's approach) had been predicted in the Old Testament Scriptures.

The greatest disaster that the Jewish nation had had to face in Old Testament times was the exile in Babylon. One of the great prophets, Isaiah, had both predicted the exile and said that the people would one day be returned to the land of Palestine (Isaiah 40 and onwards). However, sometimes Isaiah's words seem to describe a deliverance not just of the Jews from Babylon but of the whole world from sin (e.g. 49:6; 51:4–5). This is typical of the predictions of the prophets. While they spoke of events in the near future, they often suggested that the prophecies pointed forward to yet greater events of which the earlier experiences were but pale shadows.

Thus the people did return from the exile, as Isaiah had

predicted, but their experience was never as extraordinary or as wonderful as Isaiah had described it: something more amazing was anticipated. Matthew saw that the predictions of a herald who would advance before God himself (Isaiah 40:3–5) could only be true of John, the baptizer. John even fulfilled the most unlikely part of the prophecy. No preacher in his right mind goes to uninhabited places to make his addresses! But John had proclaimed his messages in the wilderness of Judea: a vast deserted area each side of the River Jordan and the Dead Sea.

Repent!

A herald's task is to ensure that everyone is ready for the arrival of someone far greater than himself. This is exactly what John did. John's message was straight to the point; not the sort of message most people would want to hear! He challenged people directly and warned his hearers that they needed to get right with God.

To understand fully what John demanded we need to know what he meant by the 'kingdom of heaven' (verse 2). The Old Testament looked forward to a time when God would establish his rule over the whole earth. This was described as the 'kingdom of God' or 'heaven'. This kingdom, John said, 'is near': God was about to act in a decisive way. John emphasized that men and women needed to be ready to enjoy God's kingdom for themselves, and that they couldn't just slip into it without any action or effort of their own. Above all, they must repent.

Repentance is not remorse. There are all sorts of reasons for sorrow. We may have been caught, or suffered for our actions, or others may have been hurt. But we are not necessarily sorry for what we have done. However, repentance is sorrow caused by the knowledge that we have offended God, and it leads to a determination to live a life which pleases God in the future. It involves a change of mind, leading to an 'about-turn' in behaviour. Great blessings were about to be bestowed by God; but men and women must be ready. When Jesus preached, his message was identical (Matthew 4:17), except that he taught that these blessings were to be found in knowing him (Mark

1:15; Matthew 13:16–17). In Jesus, the blessings predicted by John had begun to arrive!

Questions

1. What is the evidence that you should expect in your life to demonstrate you have truly repented?
2. How does your church emphasize the necessity of repentance when the gospel is preached? Is it over- or under-emphasized? How can the balance be kept?
3. What lessons can we learn from John's methods of reaching people with the truth?

The nearness of the kingdom

Was God's kingdom and judgment really as near as John seems to have thought? Nearly 2,000 years have since passed, and God's final judgment and Jesus' second coming are still in the future. The Bible itself provides the following information.

- The two comings of Jesus are sometimes described as though they are one event, even though the two are elsewhere distinguished. Jesus' ministry began the events which will lead to the judgment.
- The fall of Jerusalem, which took place only forty years later, is seen in the New Testament as foreshadowing the certain judgment of God (see chapter 24).
- Unbelief has a tendency to harden people. For such people judgment is truly 'at the door'.
- God's timescale is different from ours. As Peter says, 'With the Lord a day is like a thousand years' (2 Peter 3:8).

However, none of these points completely answer the problem

raised by this passage. Probably John meant that when Jesus came, those who were unable to recognize who he was would place themselves (in a special way) under God's judgment. Persistent unbelief would lead to God deserting them.

Matthew 3:4–10

True and false repentance

God looks for genuine sorrow for sin in those who would claim to be his disciples.

In Old Testament times God spoke to his people through prophets. However, there had been no prophets since the death of Malachi, about 400 BC. The Jews believed that, when God was about to set up his kingdom, he would use prophets once again. Matthew demonstrates that John was a prophet! John, like some of the earlier prophets, dressed in a distinctive way (see Zechariah 13:4; 1 Samuel 28:14; 2 Kings 1:8). His words confirmed his dress. People travelled miles to hear him, and many acted upon his message, recognizing what he was.

When people returned, John baptized them by immersing them in the waters of the Jordan River. Baptism was a common rite in the ancient world and often symbolized purification or entry into a new society (there were many 'secret societies' and other groups in the ancient world which used such practices to welcome new members). Baptism was the way people showed that they had responded to John's preaching, and it was a sign of being cleansed from sin to prepare for the kingdom which God was about to set up through Jesus. Jesus later baptized people, following John's practice (John 3:22; 4:1), and baptism became the sign of commitment to him, and the stamp on the entry-pass into his kingdom (Matthew 28:18–20; Romans 6:4).

Changed life

There were two very important religious groups in Israel at this time: Pharisees and Sadducees. Members from both these groups came to John and asked him for baptism. We might have expected John to have been delighted. However, John was both angry and suspicious about their claims to have repented. Perhaps they thought it was enough simply to be baptized in order to be accepted by God as his people. John, however, emphasized that true repentance will mean a changed life. Even today, many people believe that baptism alone makes them God's people. However, baptism is only meaningful in the response of someone who repented of sin and wishes to live to please God. It is the first step of obedience and shows the reality of our repentance.

In verse 7 John attacks the problem of the Pharisees and Sadducees vigorously. The snake was a symbol of wickedness to the Jew; it was a serpent or snake that had first deceived the human race and led to sin entering the world. These two groups would have been horrified to have been called 'a brood of vipers'. But John wanted to shock them out of their folly, and to show them that they had deceived themselves and were unaware of the very real danger that they were in. The problem with both these groups was that they both believed that God was especially pleased with them because he had made many promises to the first members of their race, and they thought that their ancestors had, by their good deeds, built up a balance with God that they could now draw on.

John stresses (verses 9–10) that God's favour carries a responsibility with it and his saving promises are not unconditional. Repentance is the only ground for acceptance with God.

Questions

1. What significance does Christian baptism have for you?

2. What do you think the church should look for in those who come forward for baptism, and in parents and godparents of children presented for baptism?
3. Do you think that modern preachers should ever preach like John (verses 7–10)? If so, where? to whom? and under what circumstances?

Pharisees and Sadducees

The origins of these two groups are shrouded in the mists of history. However, we know that the Pharisees rejected the contamination of other cultures and customs, and insisted upon a strict outward obedience to God's laws. They were so concerned to protect God's laws from being broken that they added many rules and regulations which, they thought, would stop anyone from becoming defiled. They tended to be proud and self-righteous, and despised those who did not share their convictions.

The Sadducees were very different. They accepted only the first five books of the Old Testament as God's words, and they did not believe in resurrection like the Pharisees. They enjoyed power and were willing to compromise to gain it. They were rich and powerful; the High Priest and his family were members of the Sadducee party.

God's wrath

When the Bible speaks of God's wrath, it does not mean that he loses his temper or flares into a rage. Rather, it refers to his hatred of all evil and wickedness.

God's wrath rests upon every human being, because no-one is able to live up to God's standards (Ephesians 2:3). It is experienced in this life (John 3:18, 36; Romans 1:18), although the full display of his wrath is reserved for the future (Ephesians

5:6; Colossians 3:6; 2 Thessalonians 1:8–9 and Revelation 14:10), and it is connected with the return of Jesus (Malachi 3:2–3; 4:1, 5). Without genuine repentance and trust in Jesus, men and women cannot escape God's wrath.

Matthew 3:11–17

The heart of the matter

Jesus is God and the baptizer with the Spirit, yet he agreed himself to undergo baptism.

The crowd believed John to be a prophet. However, John told his hearers that he was like a slave, whose task in ancient Palestine was to carry his master's shoes. John then made an even more astonishing claim. The idea of 'the greater or powerful one' was used in the Old Testament to refer to God himself (Daniel 9:4; Jeremiah 32:18). When God's Christ comes, John said, he will not be a mere man, as John was, but God!

There would also be a vast difference between John's work and the task of the Christ. The Christ would baptize with the fire of the Holy Spirit. True repentance and a spiritual life require a strength and power which human beings lack. However, the Christ would provide it. John could only administer the sign of repentance; the Christ would effect true repentance and holiness in men and women.

These words were finally fulfilled on the Day of Pentecost. From that day onwards, the Holy Spirit was given to all God's people. His work was seen in their lives: lives of daily repentance and holiness. There is, however, another side to Jesus' baptism with fire. Those not purified by his baptism would be consumed (verse 12). Jesus came to bring life, but those who refuse him will, one day, know him as judge. John 3:16–21 teaches a similar lesson.

Jesus is baptized

John knew enough about Jesus to believe that he should not baptize him. How could sinful John baptize one who did not need cleansing? The reason that Jesus insisted on baptism, however, may have been to reassure John (compare verses 16 and 17: John could have had few doubts after what is described there!). Or, Jesus may have wanted to show that he was willing to identify with sinners and take their judgment. His gentle reply (verse 15) may suggest this.

However, the great climax of these verses is found in verses 16 and 17. The dove was a symbol of purity and graciousness in the ancient world but, more important than this, is the fact that the Spirit appeared in a visible way and came to rest on Jesus. This confirmed that Jesus was now set aside and equipped for his ministry, and that he would be able to baptize with the Spirit.

Something even more amazing happened next (verse 17). The voice of God the Father spoke and declared Jesus to be the Son of the Father: Jesus was God, just as John had predicted the Christ would be! God is holy, and he must hate and judge sin. However, he is also the God of love. In love, he sent his Son to save men and was delighted and thrilled with the work that he was going to do.

One final point. In verses 13–17 we learn that the Father is delighted in the work of the Son and that the Spirit comes to assist Jesus with his work. Thus Father, Son and the Holy Spirit are in active harmony in seeking to save sinners! What a wonderful privilege this is.

Questions

1. How would you describe Jesus to a friend?
2. The work of the Holy Spirit is vital to the true believer. How does your fellowship explain the importance of this to its members? Does the emphasis agree with that of the present passage? If not, why not?

3. How do you think non-Christians can be helped to understand the love of God in Jesus?

The baptism with the Holy Spirit

The phrase 'baptism in the Holy Spirit' is widely used today. Often it is used to refer to experiences subsequent to conversion. However, New Testament references to the 'baptism with the Holy Spirit' (Matthew 3:11; Mark 1:8; Luke 3:16; John 1:33; Acts 1:5 and 11:16) all make it clear that the initial experience of a Christian is in mind. The use of the word 'baptism' further confirms this, as it was a word drawn from the initiation ceremonies of ancient societies, something that accompanied the *beginning* of a commitment. Baptism with the Spirit is, thus, one of the New Testament ways of describing the event of becoming a Christian. It emphasizes, in particular, that a true Christian is indwelt by God and equipped to live a holy, godly life.

A rich variety of other spiritual experiences are enjoyed by believers in the days and years which follow the time they become Christians. It is inappropriate, however, to describe them as the 'baptism with the Spirit'.

The Son of God

Many false teachings have been based upon the words 'This is my Son'. The greatest error is to think that this means that Jesus was not really God, or that he was 'born' in heaven some time 'after' his Father. John 1:1–3 shows that this is not so.

However, a son shares the same nature as his father. A man is human and his children are human. God is God and Jesus is the son. When the Bible speaks of 'God's son' it means that he shares the same nature as the Father: he is God! Matthew's readers would have understood this to be the claim made about Jesus in this passage.

Matthew 4:1–11

Put to the test

Jesus' newly revealed calling as the Son of God is severely tested by the devil.

Jesus was prepared to identify himself with all the needs of sinners (3:13–17). He was also tempted and suffered like us. But his temptation was unique; it was his calling as the 'Son of God' that was tested. These events followed immediately the marvellous experience of chapter 3:16–17; the word 'then' emphasizes this. We are often at our most vulnerable after a great spiritual experience or victory. This was also true for Elijah (1 Kings 18 and 19) and Jesus. Matthew says it was God's Holy Spirit who took Jesus to the place of testing. It was part of God's plan for Jesus to make him 'perfect through suffering' (Hebrews 2:10). Temptation is often God's way of making us grow. However, although God allows us to be tempted, Matthew emphasizes that the lure to evil was the work of the devil.

Jesus was not only tempted at the end of forty days (verses 2–3) but throughout the entire period (see Luke 4:1–17). There was no quick escape from his trials. Often the same is true for us.

In the first temptation, the devil alludes to the experience of 3:17 and seeks to undermine Jesus' confidence in the Father's words with an 'if', and encourages Jesus to put the claim to the test. The creation of doubts, especially about things to eat, had been tried by the devil before (Genesis 3:1–6). There Adam and Eve failed the test. Here Jesus passes 'with flying colours' by confidently trusting God and his word and reminding the devil that God is not to be trifled with (by quoting Deuteronomy 8:3). The devil's tactics do not change; neither do the means to overcome him!

The devil was not finished with Jesus. This time the devil

himself quotes Scripture (Psalm 91:11–12) and encourages Jesus to put the word of God to the test. It is probably significant that this confrontation is on the temple roof; the temple was the place where God lived. Surely God would care for his Son when he was so nearby and able to help, and what better place to do something spectacular and draw a crowd of followers! Jesus once again answers by appealing to the Bible. Jesus knew that Psalm 91 promised God's protection to his children but he quotes Deuteronomy 6:16: God is not to be used for experiments. Jesus knew the Bible and knew also how to interpret it accurately and, in this way, he overcame the devil. The lesson for us ought to be obvious.

Jesus' third temptation probably took place in a vision which enabled the devil 'in an instant' (Luke 4:5) to show Jesus 'all the kingdoms of the world and their splendour'. The temptation was, however, no less real. The devil offered Jesus earthly power instead of spiritual authority. The price of such riches was that Jesus should recognize the devil as his spiritual leader and offer him worship. Jesus saw the issue clearly and again appealed to the Bible (Deuteronomy 6:13); only God should be worshipped.

The devil eventually left Jesus (verse 11), as he will leave us.

Questions

1. Do I know the Bible well enough to face the devil's temptations when they come? Collect any verses/passages that will help you (this can be a long-term project).
2. What comfort should the fact that Jesus experienced such trials bring to you when you are tempted?
3. What does this passage teach about spiritual warfare? Is this teaching consistent with the teaching you receive in your fellowship?
4. To what extent does this passage help to explain the world we experience and live in?

Matthew 4:12–25

On the move

Jesus' public ministry begins. His teaching and healing reveal who he is. How should people respond?

Jesus' ministry began when John's work had come to an end (verse 12). His base in Galilee was the strategically important town of Capernaum.

However, the importance of Capernaum to Matthew was that it had been allocated to the tribes of Zebulun and Naphtali after the conquest of Canaan; of these two tribes, one of the most remarkable prophecies of the Old Testament had been made (Isaiah 9:1–2).

For centuries, the people living in northern Israel had suffered political and military aggression as wave upon wave of enemy attacks had been made from the north. The language of Isaiah's prophecy reflected this situation. But those same people, he said, would one day be the first to experience something very different, and darkness would be exchanged for light. In the Bible light is often used as a picture of laughter and life lived to the full, and it is especially used to speak of the knowledge and the presence of God. This prophecy, Matthew believed, was fulfilled as Jesus began his ministry, proclaiming the dawning of the kingdom of heaven.

Like John, Jesus' own words (verse 17) made it clear that only those who knew they had sinned against God, who were under his judgment, and had turned in repentance to him, had any hope. But for those who did come to him, however poor, distressed and needy (as Galileans certainly were), there was good news indeed!

The first disciples

At this point Jesus invited four men to join him. In ancient Palestine it was usual for disciples to gather round a teacher. Here, however, Jesus calls them to him. This emphasizes his authority; those he called were expected to follow him. But Jesus was no schoolteacher simply feeding his students with information; to follow him was to join him in the work of calling men and women to repentance and faith. For us, as for Peter, Andrew, James and John, this may mean giving up our livelihood and putting close family ties second. Jesus deserves nothing less.

The last three verses of the chapter form a bridge to chapters 5:1 – 9:34. They describe the nature of Jesus' ministry. Jesus did three different things: he taught the Bible when invited as a visitor to speak in the synagogue meetings; he preached the good news of the kingdom of heaven (see also verse 17); and he did many acts of healing. As we shall see in chapters 8:1 – 9:34, these healings were intended to teach three things: they confirmed Jesus' message (compare John 14:11), they showed that he was indeed the Messiah of prophecy (look up Isaiah 35:5; 53:4–5; 61:1; Matthew 11:2–6), and they proved that with his ministry God's kingdom had begun to arrive.

Not surprisingly, Jesus' ministry caused a great stir throughout all Galilee and beyond.

Questions

1. What do you think you should learn from the response of the first four disciples to the invitation of Jesus? Does Jesus usually expect us to break professional and/or family ties? If not, how do we know when it might be appropriate to do so?
2. What does this passage teach about the way the church ought to evangelize and disciple people?
3. Where today might we find people who could be described by the words in verse 16? How can we help our contemporaries, who see religion as a descent into darkness, to find Jesus as 'light'?

Introduction to the Sermon on the Mount (5:1 – 7:29)

Getting started on the greatest sermon ever preached

In chapter 4:23–25, Matthew emphasized that teaching was the vital part of Jesus' ministry. Here he gives us a detailed account of Jesus' first great public address.

There are four popular ways of viewing Jesus' words:

- Jesus provides only standards of morality. There are two difficulties with this view. First of all, it does not work, because men and women cannot naturally live up to the standards set out here, however good they are. Secondly, this view ignores the 'beatitudes' (5:3–9), which emphasize that the renewal of a person's character comes before obedience to Jesus' words.
- Another view suggests that Jesus' words are irrelevant today, that he is setting up rules for acceptance with God which he later abandoned as unworkable. But Jesus is not setting a standard for salvation by personal effort. Rather, he is seeking to show how those who are in a right relationship with God are to live.
- Others suggest that the sermon is a standard for 'special' Christians. The problem with this view is that 5:1–2 shows that Jesus was teaching all his followers – not a special band of them.
- There is only one view which is satisfactory. Jesus here sets out the standard of Christian discipleship. All true believers are expected to provide evidence of their citizenship by living according to the Sermon on the Mount. If they do not do so, there is no real evidence that they are true believers at all.

It is helpful to compare the last two views. The first of the two assumes that a claim to be saved by Jesus is enough. But many who claim to be Christians do not live according to the standards set here. The second view emphasizes that these are standards of God's kingdom. Those who consistently fall short of the standards or who hardly try to keep them need to question whether they really are Christians.

Summary

When we understand the sermon in the way outlined above, we can summarize its message as follows:

Chapter 5:3–10 gives an outline of Christian character.
Chapter 5:11–12 shows how the proof of a genuine Christian character is seen by its reaction to the ungodly world.
Chapter 5:13–16 shows how a Christian will conduct himself or herself in society and the world.
Chapter 5:17–48 shows how a Christian will respond to the law of God.
Chapter 6:1–34 shows how a Christian will live in view of the character of God.
Chapter 7:1–27 indicates how a Christian will always live under the judgment and the fear of God.

Two difficulties

There are two difficulties usually raised when comparing Matthew's account of the sermon with that in Luke. First, in Luke 6 the sermon is said to have been given on a plain (Luke 6:17). Here in Matthew, the sermon is given on a mountain. There need not be a contradiction here. Luke could be referring to a mountain plain or Matthew could mean the hill country.

Secondly, many point to the apparent differences in the content of the sermon as recorded in Matthew and Luke. But it is not surprising that Matthew included various matters that were of special interest to him, whereas Luke did the same with other teaching.

There seems no good reason to suppose that Jesus did not preach all this material on one occasion, especially if it was taught over several days. The fact that some of his teaching occurs in different settings in other gospels merely suggests that Jesus sometimes used the same material more than once (as all preachers do!).

Matthew 5:1–6

Right attitudes

Humble trust in God, complete dependence on him, gentleness and purity, are the marks of a true disciple.

After Matthew's introduction (verses 1–2), Jesus begins his sermon by providing an outline of authentic discipleship (verses 3–12). Each statement begins with the word 'blessed', a word which is found in many of the Old Testament psalms. It means 'O how rewarding is such a life!' and is a word especially used of those of whom God approves. The true disciple is to be envied.

The poor in spirit

The 'poor in spirit' are not the dispirited, or those who lack God's Holy Spirit or lack spiritual awareness. Rather, they are those who are convinced of their own spiritual poverty, their total inability to please God by their own merits and are trusting in God alone. Thus, in the Old Testament the word 'poor' means those with little or no earthly resources who are utterly dependent on God. Indeed, the word came to have the same meaning as righteous (note how the poor and the broken in spirit are mentioned in parallel in Isaiah 61:1; Proverbs 16:19; 29:23; Psalm 34:18). Without this attitude no-one can enter God's kingdom.

Those who mourn

Verse 4 is closely related to the previous verse. A man who is 'poor in spirit' will naturally be a man who mourns for sin, personal failure in a grief which has come from a sense of having alienated God. David, in Psalm 51, gives us a perfect illustration when he says, 'Against you, you only, have I sinned and done what is evil in your sight' (verse 4). The word used here was the strongest word for 'mourn' available to the New Testament writers. Jesus, therefore, gives us a picture of a person always conscious of his or her offence against God. But comfort is available for those who mourn. Apparently Jesus is speaking of the comfort available to the person who knows that, in him, sin may be forgiven.

The meek

Verse 5 follows on naturally, since the person who is 'poor in spirit' and who 'mourns' will also be a person who is meek. Meekness does not mean either a naturally nice person or someone who is weak, flabby, easygoing or lazy; a meek person is often firm and strong, as was Moses (Numbers 12:3).

In fact, the word 'meek' was one of the great words of the ancient world, and Jesus fills it with additional meaning. Meekness referred to the person who held a balance between too much and too little anger, who did not bear resentment and was not self-seeking. Meekness also referred to someone who is trained to obey a word of command. So when Jesus uses the word 'meek', he means someone who is obedient to God and his word, who is controlled by God's will and absolutely committed to the cause of God. A meek person is humble, recognizes personal ignorance and weakness, but also acknowledges the all-sufficiency of God.

The promise of the land of Canaan was central to the Old Testament believers. In the prophets, however, that promise was extended, and we are told that one day all God's people everywhere will live in a renewed heaven and earth. It is this great Bible truth that Jesus has in mind here.

something else. Jesus refers to the enjoyment of God's presence in his kingdom for ever.

The peacemakers

For many of us, 'peace' means the ending or the absence of hostility. In the Bible, however, 'peace' means much more, and includes wholeness, completeness, satisfaction, joy and happiness. A 'peacemaker' is, therefore, someone who promotes and encourages all that makes for God's glory and for harmony between men. This is Jesus' point in verse 9.

A 'peacemaker' should be seen at work everywhere, seeking peace within a family, active in the life of the church and working for peace in the world. Above all, a 'peacemaker' works for the spiritual good of all, following the example of his Father (Hebrews 13:20; 2 Corinthians 5:20) and Saviour (Philippians 2:1–11; Colossians 1:20). Jesus says that the 'peacemaker', and only he, will be owned by God in the final judgment. God is a God of peace. The 'peacemaker' shows that he is the child of God living in and for peace.

Verse 9 links with verse 8, and emphasizes one of the most important truths of the Christian faith. When a person becomes a Christian, a great change takes place. It may only take place gradually, but a change does take place since the Holy Spirit is given to the believer to live a godly life.

Questions

1. What evidence of the Holy Spirit's activity in your life do you most cherish? Is it the same as the evidence Jesus most loves to see?
2. What ambitions does the church today often put in place of the pursuit of holiness and peace?
3. What evidence of the Spirit's presence among believers is most likely to convict non-Christians today?

Matthew 5:10–12

Watch out! Persecution's about!

Jesus concludes the beatitudes by emphasizing the inevitability of opposition and showing how the believer is to find comfort in such an experience.

These verses begin with the final 'beatitude' (verse 10); this is explained more fully in verses 11 and 12, which teach how unbelievers will react to true Christians. Verses 13–16 are then added to provide a contrast. There the Christian reaction to and in the unbelieving world is described.

Jesus teaches that true believers will always be persecuted. He emphasizes this fact in three ways: persecution, he says, is an evidence of citizenship in God's kingdom; he speaks of 'when' (not 'if') persecution will happen; and, finally, reminds his hearers that the inevitability of persecution is a lesson supported by history (verse 12).

The persecution Jesus had in mind here is being ill-spoken of (verse 11). Very often, of course, Christians have to experience worse persecution than this, but all believers must experience this least form of persecution at some time or another.

Sometimes Christians suffer because of their sin, their own stupidity, folly or falsely-directed zeal, or they suffer because of party-spirit. Jesus is not thinking of any of these things here because he refers only to persecution 'because of righteousness' or 'for my sake'; persecution which arises because of a person's right beliefs or good conduct. Today, unbelieving men and women are often ready to ridicule the person who practises Christian love and forgiveness, or the Christian who, in her or his place of work, insists on doing a full day's work and refuses to tell lies.

Despite all this, Jesus tells us that persecution is not simply to be endured but is to be made the ground for the greatest rejoicing (verse 12). There are several reasons for this: persecution gives us evidence that we really are Christians (verse 10), and offers increased assurance that we are God's children. The reward which Christians will one day obtain is not to be compared with the experience of persecution now (again verse 12).

Questions

1. What encouragement can you gain from this passage as you think back over some of the difficulties that others have created for you because you claimed to be a Christian?
2. What difficulties has your church experienced at the hands of non-Christians? Why?
3. Why do you think the church in the West today seems rarely to experience persecution?

Matthew 5:13–16

Salt and light

Jesus describes some of the responsibilities of those who want to follow him.

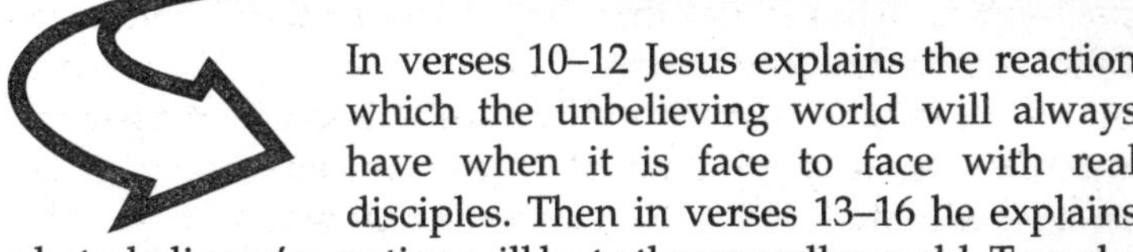

In verses 10–12 Jesus explains the reaction which the unbelieving world will always have when it is face to face with real disciples. Then in verses 13–16 he explains what a believer's reaction will be to the ungodly world. To make this point, Jesus uses two illustrations: salt (verse 13) and light (verses 14–16).

Throughout the world the main use of salt is to prevent decay.

Jesus, therefore, teaches here that the unbelieving world, left to itself, has a tendency to more and more sin and wickedness. Morally, people can only go from bad to worse unless 'salt' intervenes. Very often in the history of the world, nations and peoples have been morally transformed when true believers have been most visible. Of course, when rubbed in as a preservative, salt cannot be seen; it is invisible but still at work. Jesus teaches that consistent disciples can prevent sinful decay and have a powerful effect on the world – even if it is invisible.

To be effective salt must not be polluted. So a true disciple will keep himself or herself from being polluted and will seek God's will and glory in everything. This does not mean avoiding all contact with the unbelieving world. A disciple can only be salt as he or she mixes with unbelievers! How? First, salt is a preservative (see above). Secondly, salt gives flavour. A consistent disciple will display a quality of life which others lack, and will show, in the enjoyment of legitimate pleasures, a quality of life which unbelievers should envy. Thirdly, salt is an antiseptic. A true disciple will seek to be pure in every area of life.

Conversely, when salt becomes polluted it is useless, and also harmful, because ground tainted by it becomes sterile. Thus, a disciple who is not like salt is a bad example to others. And, most serious, is Jesus' question 'how can it be made salty again?' These words not only teach the impossibility of a true disciple living a useless life, they also imply that such a person faces inevitable judgment and rejection by God. We must be salty.

When Jesus added, 'You are the light of the world', he taught that there can be no such thing as 'a hidden disciple' but that a disciple's genuineness will be seen in lifestyle. It is not merely in a person's words, in his or her actions or 'good works', that authentic Christianity will be seen. These 'good works' include right, beautiful and attractive actions, done in such a quiet way as to draw attention to God alone.

Questions

1. Jesus describes here a life which cannot avoid being a witness to God. It is a life which inevitably is found in all true

disciples. To what extent do you think that it is true of you? How might you improve?
2. In what ways do you think the church today ought to be engaged in 'good works'? What dangers are there in over-involvement in social work?
3. How can we communicate to non-Christians that 'good works' cannot save them?

Matthew 5:17–20

The Old Testament law today

Jesus explains how we are to understand and interpret the Old Testament law in our own situations.

This is one of the most frequently debated and misunderstood passages in the Bible. It is vital to look at it closely to be sure that we know what it means.

Jesus told his listeners that his teaching was in complete agreement with the whole of the Old Testament (verses 17–18), but that it was very different from the interpretation of the teachers of the law and the Pharisees (verses 19–20).

For the Jews, the 'law' referred to the laws in the books of Genesis to Deuteronomy, 'Prophets' meant the books from Joshua to 2 Kings (excluding Ruth), and Isaiah to Malachi (excluding Daniel), and the other books of the Old Testament were known as 'the Writings'. However, the words 'law and prophets' usually apply to the whole of the Old Testament. This seems to be Jesus' usage here: he thus teaches that he does not destroy any of the Old Testament teachings. The word 'fulfil' does not mean to add or to replace but expresses the ideas of obedience and completeness. So Jesus claims that the whole of the Old Testament pointed to him and that he completely obeyed all of it.

Jesus spoke Aramaic. The Old Testament Scriptures were written in Aramaic and Hebrew, and both these languages had the same alphabet. The 'jot' (see AV) was 'the smallest letter' (verse 18) of the alphabet. The 'tittle' (see AV) was 'the least stroke of a pen' on any letter. In this way, Jesus teaches he has no intention of changing any of the Old Testament. A great deal of discussion has occurred on the word 'until' (verse 18). However, it is a word which simply emphasizes permanence. Jesus teaches that the Old Testament is permanent and unchanging in its basic lessons.

Righteousness explained

In verses 19–20 Jesus answers the other question, 'What is true righteousness?' The teachers of the law and the Pharisees taught the importance of obeying all the Old Testament law. Thus, they wanted to be faithful to all God's laws, as Jesus knew (this explains his words in verse 19). However, there were two big flaws in their understanding of the Old Testament law. First, they emphasized ceremonies and outward conformity to God's law and placed little emphasis upon loving obedience from the heart. This is why Jesus says in verse 20 that true righteousness is greater than that of these men. Secondly, the teachers of the law and the Pharisees added so many rules that many of the great lessons of the Old Testament were lost and, sometimes, even denied. In verses 21–48 Jesus discusses this particular fault in detail.

In these verses Jesus, therefore, teaches that the Old Testament and, especially its standard of righteousness, remains the standard for acceptance with God and the standard of conduct expected of citizens of his kingdom. Jesus knew that nobody (except himself, verses 17–18) could fully obey the law, and that was why he became a man (see 1:21). The problem with the teachers of the law and the Pharisees was that they thought that they could do all that was required for acceptance with God. Jesus' teaching denies this. No-one can ever do what God requires, nor can anyone ever fully obey God's laws from the heart. But God does look for lives that, with his help, come as near as possible to full obedience to his law.

Questions

1. Have you the same interest in the Old Testament Scriptures as Jesus? If not, why not? Write for yourself a scheme for reading at least a part of each Old Testament book in the coming twelve months.
2. Should our churches preach the law or preach Jesus' own lifestyle and conduct? What are the differences?
3. To what extent do you think non-Christians understand the law in a similiar way to the teachers of the law and the Pharisees? How far do you notice that understanding *within* your church too?

Understanding Matthew 5:21–48

Four main points are made by Jesus in this section of his sermon.

- He emphasizes that the moral principles of the Old Testament laws remain God's abiding standards for mankind.
- He teaches that the Old Testament laws were not a complete list of rules nor were ever intended to be. They were examples of how God's will applied to specific situations and were intended to show how to apply the great principles of the Old Testament. The teachers of the law and Pharisees failed to understand this and, by concentrating their attention on the laws themselves, they had lost sight of the great principles which lay behind them.
- He emphasizes that the teachers of the law and Pharisees had not understood that obedience to the law included

motives, desires and the intentions of the heart.

- He shows that, although the laws in the Old Testament were usually prohibitions, they were intended to prompt people to be positive. The teachers and Pharisees had entirely failed to notice this.

The first verse of every new section in chapter 5:21–48 begins with words like 'You have heard that it was said to the people long ago . . . But I tell you . . .'. In saying this, Jesus is comparing the interpretation that the teachers of the law and the Pharisees had made of the Old Testament law with the true one which he was to give.

Matthew 5:21–26

God hates hatred!

It is not simply murderous actions but murderous thoughts that arouse God's anger.

Jesus quotes Exodus 20:13 and the addition which the teachers of the law had made to that law when they said: 'And anyone who murders will be subject to judgment.' He then criticizes them not only for what they said but for what they left unsaid or unemphasized. And he does so by appealing to his special authority as the Son of God. This was not what the Jews were used to. The teachers of the law and Pharisees were always appealing to other people's opinions.

The law which prohibited murder was intended to teach the sanctity of life. This principle is found in Genesis 9:1–7, which teaches that God alone has rights over life, so when someone takes another life this is a wanton disregard of God. In

Genesis 9:1–7 there is also another idea. Mankind is made in 'God's image', a fact which gives every human being great dignity. It follows from this that to murder another person is to deface God's image. In fact, anything that does not take another person's sanctity and dignity seriously is wrong. As examples, Jesus mentions anger, contempt and slander ('Raca', verse 22).

But that is not all. Quite deliberately, Jesus twice speaks of the other person as a 'brother'. His point is this: a good family looks after the best interests of its own members (unlike Cain, see Genesis 4:9). God expects all people to do the same for one another. Anything less is disobedience to God.

Ritual no substitute for living action

It is difficult for us to understand how Jesus' words in verses 23–26 follow on from those in verses 21 and 22. Perhaps Jesus had in mind a popular objection to his teaching. There were probably those who felt that performing proper religious rituals was more important than their quality of life. But this evades God's will, as Jesus points out.

In Jesus' example, someone is offering the correct sacrifice required by God to make himself acceptable to God. However, as this man is offering his sacrifice, he remembers a person with whom he is not reconciled. Jesus says that unless an attempt is made at reconciliation, the offering is useless.

Note that Jesus does not say, 'If you have anything against a brother'. Rather, he refers to someone who is known to bear a grudge against the person making the offering. Neither does he say, 'If your brother has a good complaint against you'; the grudge might well be unreasonable! Even so, a genuine attempt at reconciliation between 'brothers' should take place or the offering will not be accepted. Thus, Jesus' words show that a prohibition in the Bible is to be interpreted and applied positively.

The last two verses (25 and 26) explain why Jesus stressed the urgency of being reconciled. If nothing is done, a relationship may get even worse.

The standards in these verses may never be perfectly achieved in this life. However, we are expected to seek to do what Jesus desires for us as far as we can.

Questions

1. Is there someone who is not reconciled with you? What are you going to do about it?
2. How might your church emphasize the importance of reconciliation, especially when the members gather around the Lord's table? Is saying 'Peace be with you' enough?
3. In a divided world, how should Christians be seeking to bring about reconciliation?

Capital punishment

In Genesis 9 the Bible emphasizes that, because life is sacred, offences against life must be treated with great seriousness. This conviction lies behind the very strict laws of the Old Testament: a person who had acted against God in taking another's life must be made seriously aware of his offence. Indeed, such a person forfeited the right to life. In the Old Testament God sometimes appointed men to act on his behalf to take the life of such people.

Today, we too should regard offences against the sanctity of life very seriously. However, we must not be legalistic. The detailed application of God's Word today will vary. Clemency and mercy are not out of place, especially where there is repentance. David was a murderer, but God forgave him and he died in peace. So, although the Old Testament laws remain valid for all time in principle, we are free to apply them in a spirit of mercy and forgiveness.

This is not inconsistent with Jesus' words about 'the smallest letter' and 'the least stroke of a pen' in 5:18, because he shows in the rest of the chapter that his concern is for the full application of the basic principles of the law, not the blind imposition of its precise rules.

War

The Old Testament permits war and the New Testament emphasizes that all of God's people have an obligation to rulers (1 Samuel 15:1; Romans 13:1ff.). However, there is no necessary conflict with the teaching here. It may seem to some believers that it is necessary for a state, in a world of sin, to go to war. The Christian has a responsibility to the state, and this may be seen to include sometimes 'lifting up a sword' against one's fellow human beings. This is not murder in the Bible, because murder is where one man deliberately kills another man out of hatred; and it is murder that Jesus is discussing at this point.

The wider question as to whether this 'just war' theory is in fact biblical cannot be tackled here. However, this passage, on its own, does not deny such a theory.

Matthew 5:27–32

Adultery and divorce

Sexual purity begins in the heart but is expressed in the permanence of marriage.

Adultery of the heart (verses 27–30)

These verses provide Jesus' second example of how the Old Testament laws should be understood and what we should understand by true righteousness.

Jesus quotes the seventh commandment (Exodus 20:14) and the

literal way in which the Jews had understood God's words, where they applied the law only to the act of adultery. In response, Jesus does not condemn an admiring look, nor the proper use of our natural and God-given sexual instincts, nor does he condemn the fiery dart of temptation which enters the mind but is speedily quenched by the child of God. He does condemn the deliberate lustful look: there is nothing innocent about the thoughts and actions of the person described in verse 28.

Jesus shows (verses 28–29) that all wilful imagination which leads to sin in the heart is wrong and needs to be put to death. The words are not, of course, to be taken literally. If Jesus had intended this, he would have mentioned both hands and both eyes! However, the eyes are mentioned as the main organ for lust, and the hand as the main organ for action. Both must be disciplined to avoid temptation.

Marriage is for life (verses 31–32)

In Jesus' third example, he looks at the attitude of the teachers of the law and the Pharisees to divorce. Jesus quotes the law which they had based on Deuteronomy 24:1–4.

To understand Jesus' words, we need to look at the main Bible passages which deal with divorce and remarriage. These are Deuteronomy 24:1–4; Matthew 5:31–32; 19:3–9; 1 Corinthians 7:12–16. There are several ways of understanding these passages.

1. It is usually suggested that Deuteronomy 24 permitted, but did not encourage, divorce; indeed the Old Testament never did *approve* of divorce. However, Jesus replaces the Old Testament teaching by a new standard. Divorce is now only possible for 'adultery' (see also Divorce and Remarriage, p. 187). 1 Corinthians 7 does not mention the word 'divorce', so it is suggested that it refers to separation which may take place following desertion. In the New Testament remarriage can only take place following the death of one's partner.

2. Another view recognizes that, although Paul does not use the word 'divorce' in 1 Corinthians 7, he does use language which clearly refers to it. To avoid a contradiction with Jesus, it is said that Jesus was speaking about marriage between

believers. Paul, however, is thinking about marriages between believers and unbelievers. So believers cannot divorce except for 'adultery' and desertion by the unbelieving spouse.

3. Perhaps the best explanation is the following one. Jesus was making no attempt to replace the Old Testament law but he was trying to meet a question which the Jews often asked, 'What are the grounds for divorce in the Old Testament?' However, he does not answer the question directly. Rather, he makes the point that they are asking the wrong question. Instead of arguing about the grounds for divorce they ought to have asked first: 'What does the Old Testament teach about marriage?' Jesus emphasized that the ideal for marriage is that of a bond which is broken only by death.

Nevertheless, he recognized that divorce was permissible in practice, and that in the case of adultery it might be undertaken without incurring the guilt of sin for the 'innocent' party. This does not mean that divorce following adultery was compulsory. Jesus would presumably not have encouraged the person whose unreasonable conduct had driven their husband or wife to adultery to be regarded as without guilt. However, Jesus made no attempt to modify the general teaching of the Old Testament that divorce may be permitted for various reasons. Paul assumes this too by offering the example of desertion.

But Jesus emphasized what the teachers of the law and the Pharisees did not. He taught that divorce is almost always sinful and requires sorrow and repentance and, if possible, restoration. In fact, the Bible seems to provide no specific grounds for divorce. We must determine whether a divorce is advisable according to the individual circumstances of the case. But we must never neglect to teach that, wherever a marriage breaks down, sin has taken place.

Questions

1. Are there temptations which I really rather enjoy thinking about? Should I be taking steps to improve in this area? How does Jesus feel about it?
2. If divorce is always 'sinful', what does this teach about the

seriousness of marriage and the care with which marriage ought to be contracted?

3. Is divorce worse than the prolonged agony of a couple living together in hatred? Why/why not?
4. Churches often get into difficulty when pastorally handling divorcees. How might this passage help resolve some of these difficulties?

Matthew 5:33–42

Swearing and going the second mile

A true disciple will always honour the truth and will not be driven to revenge.

Jesus continues to give examples of his teaching in Matthew 5:17–20. Once again he refers to a popular teaching among the Jews (verse 33). He here summarizes Leviticus 19:12; Numbers 30:2 and Deuteronomy 23:21. Again, he finds fault with the interpretation of the Jewish religious leaders, and shows that they had reversed the original intention of the law. In particular, they taught that only oaths 'to the Lord' were unbreakable.

This kind of legalistic argument becomes quite unnecessary if Christians leave oaths out of their speech. There is no need to appeal to the witness of a part of one's body or a place, much less to God himself, if one's straightforward 'yes' or 'no' means precisely that, no more and no less.

Going the second mile

In verse 38, Jesus again quotes words from the Jewish traditional interpretation of the Old Testament and shows how the Jews were wrong. The summaries of Exodus 21:24; Leviticus 24:20 and Deuteronomy 19:21 are right enough, but the Jews had not properly understood them.

In the Old Testament the instructions given (see especially Deuteronomy 19:18) were for the magistrate, and the laws were intended to provide principles upon which decisions in law should be taken. There were two reasons for this: the law was intended to regulate revenge and retaliation, and to remove punishment from the realm of personal vengeance to that of the law court.

The Jews had, however, extended the principle of the law so that it became a guideline for personal conduct. This guideline for magistrates could be used to justify vindictiveness and a desire for vengeance, even through the courts.

In contrast (verses 39–42) Jesus shows how the law should be applied. Referring to the greatest insult possible in ancient Palestine (a slap upon the cheek), he suggests that personal revenge is never right.

We need to understand Jesus' words carefully. He is not speaking literally, and does not mean that a man should never react to those who take advantage of him. For the sake of justice and the rights of others, he may and will defend himself. But the disciple is called to keep pure. A disciple should willingly endure the insults of others if he or she is the only one to be affected, and by his or her love win over the assailant.

In Jesus' day, a levy of labour could be imposed on someone by the Roman occupying forces (verse 41), and it could not be refused. The practice was no more popular than paying taxes today. Many found it extremely inconvenient and the Pharisees would have only grudgingly obeyed. Jesus' point is that this is not the standard of the disciple; duties are to be performed cheerfully and generously.

The illustration in verse 42 teaches how the disciple should react to need. In genuine cases the disciple should do everything possible to help.

Questions

1. Can you think of any situations where it might be right for Christians to tell lies?
2. What should you do when you find yourself harbouring revenge over someone else? How would you help someone who says 'I can *never* forgive him for what he has done'?
3. How can church members show that they are willing to defer to others? Where does the principle of turning the other cheek come to an end? For instance, should the church forgive a burglar who has stolen the sound system, or set the police on him? Or both?

Should Christians be pacifists?

If we understand Jesus' words in the way described in the text, we can see that Jesus is not speaking about national events. On the basis of these words Jesus did not intend to teach either pacifism or non-resistance to evil. Issues such as these require to be argued from other scriptures than these.

Neither, it would seem, is Jesus speaking about social relationships. In Romans 13 and 1 Peter 2 the relationship of the individual to the structures of society is described, and it would appear quite valid for Christians to become magistrates. It is difficult to believe that Jesus is saying that a Christian should never go to law, or not resist intruders in his house, or should recklessly dispense with his goods.

Jesus is simply teaching that, in our conduct with others, we are not to be governed by a spirit of revenge but by an attitude of love.

Should Christians swear oaths?

Some people think that they should not swear oaths in a court of law because of what Jesus says here. However, this is a misunderstanding. The Old Testament permitted and even required oaths in certain circumstances, and holy men are described in the Old Testament as taking oaths (see Genesis 14:22–24; 21:23–24; 24:3, 9; 26:31; 28:20, 22; 31:53; 47:31; 50:5; Joshua 9:15; Judges 21:5; Ruth 1:16–18; 2 Samuel 15:21; 1 Kings 18:10; 2 Chronicles 15:14–15, etc.). God also swears in the Bible (see Genesis 22:16; 26:3; Psalms 89:3, 49; 110:4; 132:11; Jeremiah 11:5; and, in the New Testament, Luke 1:73). Jesus teaches that he has no intention of setting aside anything from the Old Testament Scriptures. Jesus himself submitted to an oath (Matthew 26:63–64). So did the apostle Paul (2 Corinthians 1:23; Galatians 1:20).

Clearly, all oaths are not forbidden. Rather, Jesus is teaching that oaths are to be regulated. They should never be used lightly either to 'talk big' or in blasphemy or curse. Oaths are probably never right in ordinary conversation.

When a person makes an oath, one is going before the heavenly court and before the judge of all things. In this passage Jesus is clearly teaching that unmixed truth is the standard of the Bible. Our words ought always to be reliable and free from exaggeration. Promises should be promises.

Matthew 5:43 – 6:4

Love your enemies and do not play at religion

The greatest mark of true discipleship is selfless love for others. It is not only what you do that matters but the spirit in which it is done.

Jesus begins his final example of true righteousness and how to understand the Old Testament laws by quoting Leviticus 19:18, and the words that the teachers of the law and the Pharisees had added to that passage, 'and hate your enemy'. This interpretation overthrows the original meaning of the Bible passage, since it makes a sharp distinction between a neighbour or friend and an enemy, whereas the original law was intended to teach that love must always win over vengeance. Jesus shows that the question asked by the teachers and Pharisees, 'Who is my neighbour?' (Luke 10:36) was wrong. The neighbour is anyone in need.

The New Testament has several words for love: there is a word for love between members of a family, another for the love which exists between good friends, and another which emphasizes the sensual and sexual aspects of love between a man and a woman. Jesus, however, used another word for love which emphasized a person's will and described good intentions and helpful concern: so that, whatever a person does, however he or she treats us, insults and hurts us, we will never let bitterness enter our hearts.

Jesus gives several other reasons why a disciple must live in this way. He gives the example of God himself (verse 45). While God does have a special family love for his children (see Genesis 17:21; Psalms 103:17–18; 147:20), he also has a concern for everyone (Genesis 17:20; 39:5; Psalm 36:6; John 3:16). He expects the same of us.

Jesus gives another reason (verse 46–47); God's laws are intended to make his disciples different from unbelievers. But if God's disciples only act according to the same standards that unbelievers adopt, then there is no difference between them and there is no evidence of true discipleship.

Verse 48 concludes all of Jesus' teaching in verses 21–48. He seems to refer to Leviticus 19:2 and Deuteronomy 18:13 and teaches that the teachers of the law and Pharisees had understood these scriptures as referring to outward actions, and then only to those which the scriptures specifically commanded. In this chapter Jesus has shown that this is quite wrong. God does not want us to achieve detailed standards of behaviour by keeping carefully worded rules; he looks for a whole-hearted intention to love him and our fellow beings. Only that kind of 'perfection' makes sense.

Playing at religion (6:1–4)

In chapter 5:21–48 Jesus concentrated on the way in which the teachers of the law and the Pharisees thought. Here he is more concerned with the way they acted. His point is that, in both their thinking and their doing, they had completely failed to understand what God expected of true disciples.

A general principle (verse 1) is followed by three examples: good works (verses 2–4), prayer (verses 5–15) and fasting (verses 16–18). These three examples refer to the care that the disciple should show for his fellow men and women, for the worship he should give to God, and for the way that he should seek to root sin out of his life.

Jesus begins by criticizing all religious actions which draw attention to themselves and to the doer (verse 1). He criticizes the self-conscious actions of 'hypocrites', who merely act in front of others under the pretence of being religious.

In fact, Jesus' point is a simple one; the Jews were doing the right things but they were doing them in the wrong way. The only approval a true disciple should look for is that of God, the Father (verse 4). And when a disciple does good works to please God, God will be pleased and bless him or her in this life and in the life to come.

Questions

1. Look back over the teaching of 5:21–48. How do you fare in the 'spiritual check up' that these verses provide?
2. 'See how these Christians love one another.' Is this the view that non-Christians take of you and your church? If not, why not?
3. How does 'doing it secretly' (6:34) fit with 'letting your light shine' (5:16)?

Matthew 6:5–15

True prayer

True prayer is found in a proper attitude. Jesus gives us the supreme example of a pattern for true prayer.

Jesus now turns to prayer and probably chose it as an illustration because it is the most important of a disciple's duties to God. The Pharisees correctly believed prayer to be very important. But they were often guilty of 'play-acting' in prayer, as Jesus' two examples demonstrated. His conclusion is similar to that given in the last section: showy prayers ask for men's favour and this is what they get (verse 5). Real prayer, however, should seek only God's approval.

In verses 6–8 Jesus highlights other false prayers. Many religious people think that prayer is magical and the more prayer is offered, the more effective it will be. Some use prayer wheels and rosary beads because of this belief. Others conclude that God is impressed by fine words. Ironically, many have used the Lord's Prayer itself as an empty repetition.

Jesus, however, stresses the fact that prayer is about the heart.

God doesn't need us to babble out all the details to be sufficiently aware of our needs. The God to whom we pray is a God of love, and he is always more ready to answer prayers than people are to ask.

The model prayer (verses 9–15)

In this section Jesus provides us with a form and an example to follow (verses 9–13): it is a model of brevity and comprehensiveness.

Our Father

The word for 'Father' here is the most familiar form of the word; it means something like 'Daddy' and points to God's nearness, love and family concern for his children. The Bible does speak of God as the Father of all (Malachi 2:10; Psalm 36:6). However, in the sense that Jesus uses the word here, it only applies to the true disciple.

In heaven

This does not so much refer to where God dwells as to his power and his rule over all things. Because God is the Father in heaven this adds to the true disciple's confidence. God can do all that he wants to. Also, because he is both Father and sovereign, the proper response must include both humble confidence and reverence.

The remaining words of Jesus' prayer include six requests: three for God's glory, and three for personal needs.

Hallowed be your name

In the Bible a person's 'name' refers to all that he or she is, and to give 'honour' includes humble dependence. This request is, therefore, a plea for God to be honoured by everyone, including the one who makes the request.

Your kingdom come

Jesus taught that God's kingdom had come because of his own great acts (Matthew 12:28). When the disciple prays for God's kingdom to come, he or she prays for God to establish Jesus' authority in his or her own life and lifetime. It is a prayer that God's salvation be established in the hearts of his people.

But this prayer is also a request to see God's kingdom finally established in the age to come (look also at Revelation 22:20). Every true believer should look forward to the time when he or she will meet God, should want to see God's promises fulfilled, long for the time when 'he will wipe away every tear from their eyes. There will be no more death or mourning or crying or pain' (Revelation 21:4).

Your will be done on earth as it is in heaven

In heaven, God is always the object of praise and worship, so this request asks that God's will be obeyed completely, joyfully and immediately on earth, in the same way as it is always done in heaven.

Give us today our daily bread

We all have physical needs, and God is no less concerned about our daily needs than he is about great matters. The word 'bread' probably refers to all those things which are necessities in life; luxuries are not in Jesus' mind.

Forgive us our debts

A debt is something which is rightly owed, and Jesus recognizes that everyone is a debtor to God because of failure and sin. His prayer is for God's mercy. Because we fail daily, every true disciple often has to make this request. The person who claims to be a disciple, but who doesn't forgive others, shows that he or she is a stranger to God's forgiveness.

Just in case we miss the importance of this petition, Jesus added a few words to explain and emphasize this request after the prayer (verses 14–15).

Lead us not into temptation

Temptation itself is not sinful, but it is intended to test our strength and loyalty and ability to serve God. However (see 4:1–11), there is always an element of danger in temptation because the devil is its author. Jesus, therefore, teaches that a true disciple seeks as far as possible to avoid temptation.

Some versions of the Bible include the words, 'For yours is the kingdom and the power and the glory for ever. Amen.' These words do not seem to have originally belonged to Matthew's gospel. Among the Jews it was usual to end a prayer with words of worship. When Jesus' prayer came to be used, these words were probably added. They seem to be drawn from 1 Chronicles 29:11; Nehemiah 9:5; Psalms 145 – 150.

This prayer is comprehensive, including reference not only to God's glory (the first three petitions) but also to our own needs (the last three). It refers to physical needs (the fourth) and spiritual needs (the fifth and sixth), to present needs (fourth), needs that relate to the past (fifth) and even the future (sixth). Finally, the disciple takes to God's throne burdens that are not only his but also his brother's and sister's ('our', 'us'). All of these things are included in six brief requests. This is, indeed, a perfect pattern for our prayers.

Questions

1. Do you really want your prayers answered when you recite this prayer? If God answered you, what changes would need to take place?
2. How can public prayer in our churches become real corporate prayer, rather than a recitation of 'prayers' or a solo performance?
3. If prayer is the key to the church impacting the world, why are prayer meetings often the 'Cinderella' activity in church-life?

Persistence in prayer

Jesus does not contradict the Bible's teaching that persistence in prayer is approved by God. Jesus prayed for entire nights (Matthew 14:23–25), Paul speaks about continuous prayer (Romans 12:12; 1 Thessalonians 5:17), and Jesus himself mentions persevering prayer (Luke 11:5ff.; 18:1–8). What Jesus forbids is making form and length a basis for determining how spiritual we are.

Matthew 6:16–24

Purposeful living

First things first! Even food may be less important than God.

Proper use of fasting (verses 16–18)

Fasting, abstaining from food for a time, was taken for granted as part of a good Jew's life. Jesus does not discuss its merits, but whether it is undertaken in the right spirit. Fasting, properly used, may be an expression of our determination to get our lives into proportion and clarify our priorities.

Among the Jews there were two different types of fast. There were the public fasts where everyone took part, which took place, for example, on the Day of Atonement (see Leviticus 16) or at the time of national disaster. There were also private fasts (see Mark 2:18; Luke 18:12), undertaken as a way of normal moral and religious discipline. Jesus seems here to be speaking about private fasts, especially those which have been entered into to express humiliation. He taught that a genuine disciple was to be sincere and not showy when fasting (compare verses 17–18 with 3–4, 6).

Jesus' words may also be seen as a call to temperance (not abstinence), and the avoidance of excess where we become preoccupied with other things to the exclusion of God. It is sometimes right for a disciple to forsake legitimate things in order to be dedicated to spiritual pursuits.

Priorities in life (verses 19–24)

In 6:1–18, Jesus spoke of the danger of religious formalism. In verses 19–34 Jesus lists two other dangers: worldliness (19–24), and anxiety (25–34). Both of these dangers result from the disciple living in an unbelieving, sinful way.

Jesus' words here have often been taken to mean that a disciple should never make plans and prepare for the future (see verse 11), sometimes that poverty is especially approved by God. Neither of these conclusions are correct, since Jesus is concerned with a person's attitudes – with the heart. In fact, a poor person can be worldly and a rich man can be a true disciple.

Jesus criticizes the person who pursues those things that this world has to offer rather than living a life devoted to God. This, he says, is foolish, earthly treasures wear out, lose their attraction with age and cannot be taken into the next life. In fact, a disciple ought to be making preparations for the life to come and set on storing up treasures in heaven.

Everyone sets their hearts on what they believe to be important, and this should control their lives (verse 21).

A slave had no rights in the ancient world; he or she was the property of a master and at every moment had to do what the master required. It was impossible to have two masters (verse 24). The same, Jesus said, is true in living for God.

Questions

1. What are God's ambitions for you? Are you following them? Does self-discipline come into the picture? How do you feel about that?
2. What are God's ambitions for your church? What are those of your group? How far do they differ?
3. What place has fasting in today's church life? What might it include? Why?

Fasting in the Bible

In the Bible, fasting has many facets. It is found as an expression of humiliation (Leviticus 16:29–34; 23:26–32; Numbers 29:7–11; Deuteronomy 9:18; 1 Kings 21:27; Nehemiah 9; Daniel 9:3–4; Jonah 3:5), or took place as an act of sorrow over illness or some other disaster (Judges 20:26), or bereavement (1 Samuel 31:13; 1 Chronicles 10:11–12; 2 Samuel 1:12), or on the arrival of sad news (Nehemiah 1:3–4), a plague (Joel 1:14; 2:12–15), or when faced by threatened disaster (2 Chronicles 20:3, 5; Esther 4:3; 9:31). There was a natural basis for fasting, since overwhelming grief or distress produces loss of appetite. There were also other fasts which were ordered or observed to promote concentration in spiritual things (compare Isaiah 58, especially verses 6–12).

Matthew 6:25–34

Anxiety and how to avoid it

God is sovereign, and he loves and cares for each of his disciples. We should not be paralysed by worries about the future.

In verses 19–24 Jesus spoke about the danger of the divided heart. Here he refers to those attitudes which arise from an imperfect faith. Jesus is not telling the true disciple never to make plans for the future. After all, birds are industrious and prepare their nests (see verse 26), and the Bible teaches that we should work hard and plan (Proverbs 6:6; 2 Corinthians 12:14; 1 Timothy 5:8). No, Jesus is warning us about paralysing anxiety which can sometimes seem to occupy a person's every waking moment.

Jesus mentions the necessities of life: food, drink and clothes (verse 25), since these are very often matters for care and concern, especially in societies where there can be serious shortages. He says that natural concern must never become anxiety. He provides several reasons:

- 'Life', he says, 'is more than food and clothes' (see verse 25). The Jews often argued from a lesser thing to a greater. Jesus seems to do that here and to say that, since God has given us life, why worry about lesser things?
- Tiny birds are cared for by God without their need to get anxious (verse 26). If God cares for the birds, he must surely care for men and women.
- Anxiety is fruitless and never achieves anything (verse 27).
- Nothing is so beautiful as a field of flowers. But the flowers do not achieve such beauty by anxious care but through God's provision. If God gives such beauty to a field, Jesus says, he must certainly care for his children's needs (verses 28–29).

How then does anxiety arise? The source is a defective faith (verse 30). So, the true disciple should never worry, even if others do, but should be confident that God does know every need, and he or she should be totally absorbed in living for God. Then each day can be lived 'one day at a time'.

Questions

1. Is there something worrying you today? What encouragement can you find in this passage to face it? Does living each day 'one at a time' help?
2. What worries cripple your fellowship from living by faith? Are some Christians more naturally prone to worry than others? Does it help them to be told that they lack faith? How can you help one another in this area?

3. In the light of this passage, what difference do you think the non-Christian ought to see in a Christian?

Can a Christian ever be in need?

Some people, especially in richer countries, have used these verses to say that true disciples should never lack the necessities of life. God's disciples in poorer lands, of course, know that this is not true. So, how are we to understand Jesus' words?

In the Old Testament we find what is called 'wisdom' teaching. The book of Proverbs is the most famous 'wisdom' book. 'Wisdom' looked at life and drew general conclusions on the basis of experience, but these conclusions were not absolute rules. In fact, when these observations were made into rules, they did not work. We see this when Job's comforters tried and failed to explain Job's experience; they thought that, because he was suffering, he must have sinned, but the book of Job shows that this was not so. Suffering is often the result of sin, but it is not always so.

Jesus' words here should be understood here as 'wisdom'. They are generally, but not always, true: when God's people do suffer want and even death, it is because God has a greater purpose to achieve through them. Whichever is true for us, we can absolutely trust God.

Matthew 7:1–12

Criticize with care!

We gain nothing from criticism which is spiteful, uncaring and hypocritical. Rather, we should look to God, who provides what we need.

The habitual fault-finder (verses 1–6)

Jesus' words in verse 1 do not mean that we should always indulge other people's faults. Rather, he is referring to the sort of people who go out of their way to find fault in others and enjoy it (verse 3). It is a picture of harsh, self-righteous criticism which shows neither love nor mercy.

Such people are more concerned with others' weaknesses than they are with personal self-examination; always finding reason to criticize others but never aware of personal need. Indeed, often those very faults that a critic finds in others are most apparent in themselves, even if, sadly, they are unaware of it (verse 5). What makes it worse is the fact that it is a 'brother' who is being criticized – someone who ought to be helped. Jesus does not minimize the seriousness of the matter (verses 1 and 2): a person who is an habitual critic forfeits his citizenship in God's kingdom.

True criticism, Jesus adds, requires several things:

- A good judge needs clear vision. A blind or a near-blind optician is of no help at all! To be a brother's judge first requires self-examination, repentance and prayer to God for help (see especially verse 7).
- Criticism must be undertaken in the right way and for the other person's benefit.

- Criticism must be done with careful discrimination. Jesus is thinking of wild, large, savage and ugly dogs, and the pigs, regarded by the Jews as unclean and filthy (compare Leviticus 11:7; Deuteronomy 14:8). These sorts of people must be treated according to their condition and need.

God loves to answer our prayers

The standards set for the true disciple in chapters 5–7 are very high indeed: not least is this true of 7:1–6! Men and women cannot live up to God's standards. However, help is available from the Father (verse 11; compare 6:9), who is ever ready to give help. What the disciple is unable to do, God can do in him or her (verses 7–8). In dependence on God, the disciple is to 'ask', 'seek' and 'knock'.

Everyone who looks for help in this way will find it, and God will give in exact proportion to the need. He will provide neither a deceiving substitute nor something which will hurt rather than help. If a human parent acts in such a good way as to meet the needs of his or her children there is no doubt that God will do the same!

Verse 12 seems to act as a conclusion to 7:1–11 and for the whole of the sermon so far. It has often been understood to mean that God accepts the person who lives according to this standard. But Jesus cannot possibly mean this since, throughout the sermon (and especially in 7–11), he teaches that only the person relying absolutely on God in his helplessness is acceptable to God. Moreover, in 6:12 Jesus taught that men and women are always in need of mercy and forgiveness.

No, God expects a true disciple's actions toward others to be governed by how much the disciple loves himself or herself. Thus, his words, 'for this sums up the law and the prophets' are intended to teach that all the moral standards of the Old Testament are based on this one principle.

Questions

1. Think about someone who is inclined to criticize. How far do you recognize the same failings in yourself? (Do not hurry over this one.)
2. How can churches provide openings for constructive criticism without offending the criticized? Is it possible? How can we avoid judgmentalism?
3. How would you respond to the non-Christian who thinks that he or she is doing what is required in verse 12?

Matthew 7:13–23

Be alert!

Jesus warns us against bad decisions, prompted by a comfortable life, false informers and superficial evidence.

The narrow way (verses 13–14)

Jesus calls for deliberate decision, like Moses (Deuteronomy 30) and Jeremiah (Jeremiah 21:8) before him. He was obviously aware that, when most people are faced with a major decision, they hesitate, so he urges action.

Only a few find the way; it is not too popular and only interests a few, and it requires sacrifice. Jesus depicts something like a turnstyle which can be entered only one person at a time, and through which little luggage can be carried. Moreover, he also teaches that such effort must be continuous, for lying beyond the gate is the narrow road.

It is 'the way which leads to life' (verse 14). 'Life' in the

New Testament referred to two things: to the blessings of the age to come, where fellowship with God will be found; and to the truly fulfilled life which can be experienced in the present life. The life of a true disciple offers real pleasures, which do not tarnish even in the present age (see 6:20–23).

- Men and women are often aroused to action as much by anticipated danger as by promised blessing. While the 'broad way' encourages indecision, is the popular choice and brings much self-satisfaction it is, above all, 'the way of destruction'. Just as the narrow way leads to life, the broad way leads to death – offering both tarnishing pleasures in the present age, and the everlasting judgment of the age to come (see again 6:20–23).

The false prophets (verses 15–20)

In verses 13 and 14 Jesus called for decision in response to his message. However, he recognizes that there are others who are calling for decisions too!

False teachers are not easily distinguished from true ones. Jesus illustrates this with his words 'they come to you in sheep's clothing'. In the Bible God's people are often described as 'sheep' (not least by Jesus). False teachers may therefore claim to be true disciples. There was a thorn in ancient Palestine which closely resembled grapes, and a thistle which at a distance resembled figs. In verse 16 Jesus mentions these things as an additional illustration of the way false teachers (and their teaching) can show a casual resemblance to a true disciple.

They may look like sheep, but in reality they are something far more fearsome: strong jaws, sharp teeth and cunning characterize wolves, who attack, seize and kill their prey. The false teachers may not always be aware of their folly but, though they appear to be God's children, their teaching is always ready to work spiritual destruction on their hearers.

How then may false teachers be spotted? Jesus offers a simple test: 'By their fruits you will recognize them' (verse 16). The teaching of false prophets (compare 5:17–48) will set forward a righteousness which is external and which tends to self-righteousness. The actions of false teachers (compare chapter 6) will draw attention to themselves rather than to God's glory. False teaching will have a tendency to exalt men and women and will not seek much of God's mercy and grace.

'Cloud cuckoo land' (verses 21–23)

Jesus continues his warning against all that is false and not true religion. He offers a grim illustration of a group of self-deceived people at the final judgment who, to their considerable surprise, find that they have never been true disciples or known the path of true religion. The situation is very similar to verses 15–20 but with two main differences. In verses 15–20, reference was made to those who delude; here, to those who are deluded. There, false teachers were in mind; in verses 21–23, ordinary 'believers' seem to be mentioned.

In the final judgment these poor people are described as appealing to certain facts about themselves, believing that these facts must make Jesus receive them into his kingdom. However, the Lord's response is clear, and with great authority. Jesus tells them that these things are completely unsatisfactory grounds for acceptance with God.

What, then, do such people appeal to? They seem to claim orthodox beliefs, they show fervency and zeal, they refer to their own spiritual usefulness ('did we not prophesy in your name'), and they claim to have exercised great spiritual gifts ('. . . drive out demons'). Jesus does not deny any of these things! But they are insufficient for acceptance with God. What is lacking, says Jesus, is doing 'the will of my Father who is in heaven' (verse 21). Jesus is looking for a godly character which is outworked in a godly life – the sort of life emphasized in these three chapters (Matthew 5 – 7).

We need to learn that it is possible to be orthodox, fervent, useful and gifted and yet, without a godly character and life, never to be a true disciple, never really knowing or being known by God.

Questions

1. When I seek to reassure myself before God, what do I appeal to?
2. Where do you see the danger of (sincere but) false teaching in churches today?
3. What do these verses tell us about the 'cult of the Christian personality' in today's media? What is the value of hearing a well-known speaker? What are the dangers involved?

Matthew 7:24–29

Watch out for 'jerry building'!

Planning, preparation and forethought are needed to succeed as a disciple. Hearing God's words without obeying them is to head for disaster.

In verses 15–20 Jesus compared two groups of people: false and true teachers. In verses 21–23 another comparison was offered: mere believers and true disciples. In verses 24–27 we are provided with a final contrast between two groups: the wise and foolish builders.

Hear and do God's words (verses 24–27)

Everyone builds in life, but not all build in the same way. On the one hand there is the wise, sensible person; the sort of person who works hard, plans, follows a deliberate course. When he or she builds, this person considers all the needs and requirements and builds accordingly, and the result of such 'building' is seen in the way that they cope with sudden unexpected situations.

Generally, such a person can face such events and find a way through them.

But there is another type of builder: the foolish, unthinking person. He or she wants the same things as the wise person (a house to live in), but is not usually prepared for the hard work necessary. Such people do not make adequate plans, and are often unwilling to listen to the advice of others. Very often progress is made by the foolish person just as quickly as by the sensible person, and this seems to suggest (to them) that all planning and effort are not necessary. Unfortunately, when problems come, disaster strikes. Unprepared for difficulty, such a person's life lies in ruins.

So here Jesus describes two groups of people who want to be disciples. Only one group, however, is willing to follow God's methods. The two buildings look the same. Both groups want to be accepted by God and to be members of his kingdom. Unfortunately, beneath these similarities lie very great differences, which result from a different attitude to the word of God; one group hear and do God's will, the other only hears.

This is disastrous when trials come, since the foolish person is unequipped to face such difficulties. Even today many people who claim to be disciples of Jesus have their faith wrecked when difficulty comes. But more disastrous will be the final day of judgment: in that day such a person's claim to discipleship will not stand up under the careful examination of God.

Building on the rock of obedience to God does not mean that trials do not come. Exactly the same trials come (compare 25 and 27). However, even if the trial is worse, a strong building stands firm on well-laid foundations. Jesus clearly teaches that it is very important to know and do God's will. The final security and blessing of a disciple depends upon it.

Postscript to the Sermon on the Mount (verses 28–29)

We are told that the people who heard Jesus were 'astonished', a word which sometimes means to be amazed, overwhelmed, even sent mad! This reaction persisted for some time. What caused this? First, it was Jesus' authority; not so much by the manner of Jesus but the content of the message. When Jesus spoke, he did not say 'thus says the Lord' as the prophets had, but he spoke on his own authority. The teachers of the law and the Pharisees always quoted other people's opinions, but Jesus only gave his own. Most remarkably, in the Old Testament a prophet was God's spokesman, but in 5:11–12 Jesus claimed that his followers would be like prophets. Jesus was, therefore, claiming to be God.

Indeed, Jesus claimed things which could be true only of God: to have come (implying 'into the world' from his previous experience) to fulfil the law (5:17); to be uniquely related to God ('my Father', 7:21, compares with 'our Father', 6:9); to have the right to obedience by all (7:24); and to speak with the authority of God himself (7:21–23).

No wonder Jesus' hearers were awestruck. However, it was not only Jesus' claims that had this effect upon his hearers. It was also his teaching. In particular, he completely denied that human effort was able to make anyone acceptable to God. This was the exact opposite of what was taught by the teachers of the law and the Pharisees. He also said that obedience to God must be obedience 'from the heart'. The person God accepts must show greater holiness than that of the teachers of the law and Pharisees. That was a great shock to his hearers.

Questions

1. What is your reaction to having read the Sermon on the Mount? Take time to go back over it and ask yourself, after each section, what is God saying to me?
2. How does your church assess the genuineness of those who claim to be Christians? What in practice corresponds to 'sand' and what to 'rock' in your situation?
3. 'Jesus was a great moral teacher.' How would you answer the person who said this to you?

Matthew 8:1–4

Jesus alone can heal and forgive

Jesus heals a leper, and shows that he is the promised Messiah who brings forgiveness to men and women.

These four verses begin a new section of Matthew's gospel (8:1 – 9:34), which describes some of Jesus' miracles. Their inclusion at this point shows that Matthew carefully constructed his gospel. In 4:16 he quoted the prophet Isaiah to show that when Jesus began his work in Galilee a great light had shone out. In 4:23–25 he explained that this light was seen to shine out in Jesus' words and his acts. 5:17–20 builds upon this by showing how Jesus' words were a great light, and now 8:1 – 9:34 demonstrates the same point by describing some of his acts. The miracles described in these two chapters also confirm the authority of Jesus' words.

Miracles

What is the importance of miracles in the Bible? As we read the Scriptures carefully, we notice that miracles happened especially when God began to do something new. We read of miracles at the time of Abraham, at the time when God first entered into a special relationship with one group of people, and of great miracles in the time of Moses and Joshua when God delivered his people from Egypt and led them into the land which he had promised to them. Again, we encounter miracles at the time of Elijah and Elisha, two men who were the first of the great prophets. The lifetime of Daniel, too, was a period of miracles, at a time when God's people were especially in danger. The Jews expected that miracles would occur again when the Messiah appeared. So Matthew clearly intends us to learn that Jesus' miracles confirmed that Jesus was the Messiah (see 7:28–29). They teach that God's kingdom had arrived; that God had begun to do something new again.

In the Old Testament law, diseases are often mentioned. Many people think that these laws were only given for health reasons, but the Old Testament does not seem to have regarded leprosy as very contagious: Naaman remained the leader of the Syrian army when he was a leper (2 Kings 5:1); Gehazi, a leper, could speak to the king of Judah (2 Kings 8:4–5); and priests had to touch lepers to see if they were healed or not (Leviticus 13:12–13). In fact, many of the Old Testament laws were symbolic – intended to teach a spiritual lesson. Leprosy received special attention because it was an especially horrible disease which gradually infected the whole body. A leper was like a dead person and excluded from living with God's people.

All this symbolically taught the people of God that sin defiles people and separates them from God. This is clearly seen in the language of Psalm 51:7, where David uses the language for a leper's cleansing to ask for cleansing from sin. Among the Jews the curing of a leper was regarded as being as difficult as raising a dead person to life. Only God was thought to be able to cleanse a leper (Numbers 12:13–15; 2 Kings 5:14). However, it was believed that cleansing of leprosy would occur when the Messiah came. The belief is hinted at in Matthew 11:5. So this story confirms Jesus as the Messiah. It teaches that he is God. It clearly shows that Jesus is able to forgive sin (compare especially Mark 2:1–12).

Leprosy, a picture of sin

This poor leper seems to have understood much of this. He called Jesus 'Lord', a word which can simply mean 'Sir' but is also used in the Bible (as here?) as God's name. Since we are also told the man 'worshipped' Jesus and that he believed that Jesus could heal (and only God could do that), he showed remarkable understanding and faith, especially as he was 'full' of leprosy (Luke 5:12). Jesus' action (verse 3) confirmed the man's understanding and confidence.

Verse 4 is difficult. Why did Jesus tell the man not to tell anybody about his healing? A number of answers have been given to this question. Perhaps the words were only intended to apply until the man had showed himself to the High Priest. Jesus requested this so that there might be no hindrance to the man being declared clean. Perhaps he thought the priests would have been jealous and would not have been willing to acknowledge that the man was clean. Or perhaps Jesus commanded this so that he might not be known merely as somone who worked wonders, but as the Messiah who cleansed from sin. It is also possible that Jesus was anxious to avoid causing people to react over-enthusiastically to his ministry.

The second question raised in this verse is this, Who are the 'them' for whom this man's healing would be a testimony? It could be the crowd or the priests. If it were the crowd, Jesus' healing was a confirmation of his words. If it were the priests, it shows that Jesus recognized that his acts confirmed his ministry to those who were Jesus' opponents. This left them without excuse in opposing him.

To sum up: leprosy is a picture of individuals as sinners. Sin, like leprosy, corrupts the whole person, and it is visible in different ways reflecting the underlying sickness of the body. It also is incurable, and except for God's grace leads inevitably to death, destruction, complete separation from God's people and exclusion from the kingdom of God. But deliverance is possible. Jesus stretched out his arm to heal the leper. This was against the Old Testament law (Leviticus 5:3). A person who touched a leper became defiled, but Jesus shows that he is the one who cleanses sin. He alone can touch sin and bring healing.

There are, of course, conditions to be met. Jesus' healing power was not administered indiscriminately. Three things seem to have been required of the leper: he had to be absolutely convinced of the seriousness of his condition, he needed to be sure that Jesus as the Messiah of God was able to deal with his sin and, humbly, he needed to cast himself upon the mercy of Jesus.

Jesus looked with compassion upon this man when he came to him (Mark 1:41), and he healed him immediately and completely. Jesus never turned away anyone who approached him, and he never turns away anyone who comes to him for forgiveness from sin.

Questions

1. It is wonderful to be miraculously healed but still more wonderful to be miraculously forgiven. In the light of this story reflect upon what Jesus has done for you. Make a list or write a letter of thanks to God.
2. What place should the healing ministry occupy in the life of the church?
3. Do non-Christians need wonder-workers or preachers, or do they need both? Why?

Matthew 8:5–13

Salvation is by faith not merit

Jesus shows his followers that God's kingdom cannot be entered except through faith.

These verses contain the second miracle of Jesus recorded in Matthew's gospel. Like the leper, the centurion had faith in Jesus. He had heard about Jesus (Luke 7:3) and also seems to have meant more than 'Sir' when addressing Jesus as 'Lord', and he believed that Jesus was able to heal his servant. The particular sickness that this servant was suffering from is not known. It seems, however, to have been a case of progressive paralysis, with spasms which affected the man's breathing. This threatened his life (compare Luke 7:2).

The whole of the story told by Matthew builds up to the conversation between Jesus and the centurion. Even the miracle itself seems to take second place in the story. The centurion claims to be unworthy of Jesus' coming to his home. He must have known that Jews did not enter the homes of 'Gentiles' (non-Jews) lest they got defiled (John 18:28; Acts 10:28; 11:2–3), and he probably felt himself to be outside of the true family of God. Nevertheless his faith was clear: 'But just say the word, and my servant will be healed' (verse 8).

Jesus responded both to this faith (verse 10) and to his sense of need (verse 11). He commented on the considerable faith of the centurion as something he had not found among the Jews. Because of this faith Jesus reassured him by referring to the banquet of the Messiah to which the Jews looked forward. The Jews had misunderstood Isaiah 60:12 and believed that only they would sit down at the banquet. However, the prophets had taught that people would come from all over the world to share in God's kingdom (Isaiah 2:2–3; 11:10; 45:6; 49:6, 12; 54:1–3; 59:19; Jeremiah 3:18; 31:34; Hosea 1:9–10; 2:23; Amos 9:11–15; Micah 4:1–2; Malachi 1:11). Thus Jesus reassures the centurion in his need.

Finally, and for the benefit of the Jews, Jesus added (verse 12) that there would be those who considered themselves sure to be members of God's coming kingdom but who would find themselves destined for hell. Thus, Jesus taught the centurion that entrance to God's kingdom is by faith (verse 13): a faith which he had shown, and which was confirmed by Jesus' healing of his servant.

Questions

1. Where do I place my confidence that God will receive me? Compose a letter of application for admission to heaven.
2. Look up the Old Testament references given above concerning people coming from all over the world to share God's banquet. In what ways could or should we start celebrating God's worldwide kingdom now?
3. What implications does Jesus' teaching here have for the outcasts of society today?

The centurion

The centurion was an important person in the Roman army. Palestine was part of the Roman Empire during the time that Jesus lived. In the Roman army a legion was composed of 6,000 men and each of these legions was divided into 60 'centuries'. A centurion commanded a century and was usually a long-service regular soldier. In the New Testament, centurions are always mentioned with respect (Matthew 27:54; Acts 10:22, 26; 23:17, 24; 24:23; 27:43). This centurion would probably have been in the pay of Herod Antipas, the Roman ruler of Galilee. Capernaum was not far from Tiberias, which was Herod's base in Galilee. Since the Jews spoke for the centurion (Luke 7:3), he was probably a 'proselyte'. A proselyte was a non-Jew (known as a Gentile) who had adopted the Jewish religion.

Matthew 8:14–17

Saved to serve

Jesus' healings emphasize that he is the one whom God had sent to deal with the penalty of sin.

Matthew saw Jesus' miracles as 'acted parables' (8:1–4). In verses 1–4 Matthew emphasized that Jesus had come to heal sinful men and women, and verses 5–13 show that there were no restrictions upon those Jesus had come to save: the kingdom of God was open to all sinners who would come to Jesus humbly asking for help. Now, in verses 14–17, Matthew uses several events in Jesus'

healing minstry to teach how Jesus could save sinners (cf. 1:21).

This section begins with the healing of Peter's mother-in-law (verses 14–15). Peter appears to have come originally from Bethsaida, but according to Mark 1:29 he had a home in Capernaum. He was married (1 Corinthians 9:5) and traded as a fisherman with Andrew his brother (Mark 1:6). Perhaps his wife was from Capernaum. Certainly both families seemed to live in one house and carry out one business. Nowhere else does Matthew tell us that Jesus takes the initiative as he does here. However, when Jesus takes pity on this woman she is completely restored. Perhaps Matthew saw significance in the fact that she ministered to Jesus. Those whom Jesus saves are expected to serve him (Colossians 3:24).

Like many of Jesus' healings this event occurred on a Sabbath (Luke 4:31). This seventh day of the week was strictly observed by the Jews as a complete day of rest. The Jews said that to carry anything more than the equivalent of two figs was work! The Jews reckoned a day from sunset to sunset, so when the Sabbath had come to an end people were brought to Jesus.

In the New Testament some sicknesses are said to be the result of the devil's work (as here, verse 16). We, however, should be careful not to jump too soon to this conclusion ourselves. There are many other sicknesses that are not the devil's activity, as the last part of verse 16 shows. Matthew demonstrates that no sickness was beyond Jesus' ability to heal. Jesus healed 'all the sick'; whether 'incurable' or terminal, all were healed. But Matthew does want to show, especially, that demonic sicknesses were healed by Jesus' word. Jesus was showing his authority even over the devil (cf. Matthew 12:29; Luke 10:17; Revelation 20:2–3).

The Old Testament taught that all sickness was the result of mankind's sin (Genesis 3). This did not mean that particular sicknesses were the result of particular sins but it did mean that all were sinners. The Old Testament also looked for the time when all sicknesses (and, therefore, sin) would be brought to an end in the new creation of God. In Isaiah 53 the 'servant' (see verse 11) was described as someone who would bring all these things to pass; he would do this by bearing away sin by his death (53:11–12). He would be able to do this because he would offer himself, willingly, to bear the penalty for sin (53:10) on behalf of others (53:5). Matthew saw Jesus as the prophesied servant. Later in the gospel he will show more clearly how Jesus did take away sin.

Questions

1. If I am saved, how do I show it by my service? Write a list, not for self-congratulation but for thanksgiving.
2. How should the church counsel those who are sick? Compare the benefits of the medical profession with those of the ministry of the church. Should they work together? How?
3. Why do you think God tolerates sickness in the world (see below)? How can we explain this to non-Christians?

Should Christians suffer?

Some people take passages like this one to teach that true disciples should never suffer illnesses. If a disciple is ill, it is argued, then his or her faith is lacking.

This is wrong. First, it is inconsistent, since in the Bible there are a number of things which are the result of man's sin: pain in childbirth and 'thorns and thistles' are mentioned in Genesis 3:16 and 18. Those who argue that Christians should never suffer illness never argue that Christians should not have weeds in their gardens, nor that women who are disciples should not have pain in childbirth. It is clear, therefore, that all the results of sin are not yet dealt with.

This view also misunderstands what the Bible teaches about salvation. In the New Testament the work of salvation is incomplete, awaiting the full revelation of God's kingdom. In the meanwhile the whole of creation (including the disciple) is subject to suffering, awaiting the full revelation of God's kingdom (Romans 8:18–23). As a result of this, all men and women still suffer illnesses. Even in the Bible those men and women who healed others sometimes suffered sickness themselves, or their friends did (compare 2 Kings 13:14 and 20:1; Acts 9:36–37; Galatians 4:13; Philippians 2:25–27; 1 Timothy 5:23; 2 Timothy 4:20). Nevertheless, the Bible does encourage us to pray for healing (James 5:14–15).

Matthew 8:18–22

Jesus calls us to follow him

Jesus looks for followers who will stick to the task he gives them.

Matthew breaks off his miracle stories to tell of two conversations on true discipleship. They show us that, just as Jesus was to suffer (8:17), so must his followers (cf. 5:10–12). So it is important for everyone who wants to be a disciple to have fully counted the cost (8:18–20) and to be wholehearted in following Jesus (8:21–22).

Jesus may have felt he needed a break from the heavy demands of his work, or he may have wanted to avoid an over-enthusiastic response to his ministry. He decided to escape from the crowd (verse 18). As he did so, a teacher of the law came to him to tell him he wanted to be a disciple. Usually these teachers were hostile to Jesus (5:20; 6:2, 5, 16; 15:1) but here and in 13:52 and 23:34 we are told of those who were interested, even enthusiastic, in following Jesus. Indeed, this man said he was willing to change his way of life (verse 19). Possibly the fact that the man only calls Jesus 'Teacher' showed he had not understood who Jesus was as clearly as the leper and the centurion had. Jesus, however, tested the man's enthusiasm (verse 20). In verses 21–22 another man showed himself willing to be a disciple of Jesus. However, if the teacher of the law had not thought enough about true discipleship, this man had thought too much. He showed that he was willing to be a disciple, but he was only too aware that he had other responsibilities. In seeking to give an adequate place to his other responsibilities he ended up refusing true discipleship.

What did the man mean when he said, 'Lord, first let me go and bury my father'? Perhaps his father had recently died and the man was asking to attend the funeral. However, it is more likely that the man did not intend to be understood literally but was saying that he had responsibilities to his parents which might last for some time, and until those responsibilities were removed he couldn't be a disciple. Jesus' reply does not imply that we should ignore such responsibilities, but he does teach that responsibilities must be always held subject to the greater demands of true discipleship (10:37; 12:46–50; Ephesians 3:14–15).

Questions

1. Can you think of any demands to which you say, 'Not now, Lord, but later'? Should at least one of them not be done *now*? Make a note in your diary to do some of the others.
2. Think of some of the ways in which the church sometimes mistakes enthusiasm for faith.
3. How might these verses apply to the call to full-time Christian service?

The Son of Man

In verse 20 Jesus calls himself 'the Son of Man'. This is the first time in the gospels that Jesus calls himself by this name. In the Old Testament the 'son of man' is mentioned in several passages. In Psalm 8:4 it refers to men who are frail, powerless and utterly dependent on God. The same use of the phrase is found in the early chapters of Ezekiel. However, in Daniel 7:13 there is another reference to a 'son of man', a vague title for the

Messiah. Almost certainly Jesus intended to provoke thought and to reveal to people gradually who he really was.

This title is used twenty-nine times in Matthew's gospel: thirteen times of the coming of the Son of Man at the end of the age (e.g. 16:27; 25:31; 24:27–44; 26:44); nine times it refers to his death and resurrection and seven times, as here, to his present ministry (e.g. 17:12; 26:24; 12:40; 17:9). Here Jesus speaks about rejection: rejection began when there was no room at the inn. As the story develops, we read that Judea rejected him (John 15:18); Galilee cast him out (John 6:66); Gadara begged him to leave (Matthew 8:34); Samaria refused him lodging (Luke 9:53); earth would not have him (Matthew 27:23); and, finally, even heaven forsook him (Matthew 27:46).

Matthew 8:23–27

King of creation

Jesus' stilling of the storm raises the question, 'Who is this?'

After the short passage on discipleship (8:19–22), Matthew returns to describing some of Jesus' miracles. The earlier three miracles were seen as 'acted parables' by Matthew, designed to help to explain the work that Jesus had come to accomplish (8:1–18). These three miracles offer an answer to the question of the disciples (8:27), 'Who is this?'; to which the answer is given in 8:29: Jesus is the 'Son of God'. Jesus shows his authority over nature (8:23–27), over the spiritual realm (8:28–34) and over sins (9:1–8). As we shall see in 9:1–8, these miracles mark a turning-point in Jesus' ministry. From now on he will be pursued by the religious authorities.

Suddenly a great storm struck the boat in which Jesus and his disciples had embarked. It must have been a violent storm for Galilee, since even experienced sailors were terrified (verse 25) and Matthew uses a word that usually refers to an earthquake (verse 24). Jesus was able to sleep from exhaustion and trust in his Father, but when he was awakened he performed a great miracle: not only did he stop the wind but the waves subsided immediately (verse 26).

Jesus 'rebuked' the wind and sea. The pagan people who lived in Palestine believed that the sea was the great enemy of God. The Old Testament sometimes uses similar language (see especially Psalm 93:3–4) without accepting the pagan beliefs, teaching that the sea was subject to God (Psalm 93:4) and this would give him praise (96:11). Matthew must have seen the significance of this. The Sea of Galilee was subject to Jesus and this leads to the praise of Jesus by the disciples. This Jesus must, surely, be God.

The disciples are confident that Jesus can save them (verse 25), but could he help them while sleeping? When Jesus was awakened he rebuked a faith which depended on his presence (or being awake!), and then he performed his great miracle which showed his authority over the whole world of creation. The disciples were still not fully aware who Jesus was and they asked the question of verse 27. In a few hours they will get the answer from a most unlikely source (verses 28–34)!

This miracle is another acted parable. Unlike the men described in verses 18–22, these 'disciples' (verse 23) did 'follow Jesus'. But true discipleship is not always an easy life, and the disciples were soon faced with overwhelming difficulties. They needed to learn to live by faith in a Jesus who was in control of everything.

Questions

1. In what areas of your experience do you find it difficult to believe that Jesus can meet your need? Compare each one with the storm on the lake. Does this help?
2. What storms does your church face at the moment? How can Jesus meet the need?

3. If Jesus is Lord of creation, what does this imply about the church's responsibility to 'planet earth'?

The Sea of Galilee

The Sea of Galilee was, and is, a lake, only 13 miles in length and 8 miles wide. It is part of the Jordan valley which makes a deep cleft in the surface of the earth. Galilee is 650 feet (211 metres) below sea level. The climate is warm and friendly. However, on the west side of the lake are mountains containing deep ravines. Somtimes a wind, caught in the ravines, rushes suddenly down on the lake with great violence. The calm of one moment becomes the raging storm of the next. One observer tells of the time when he was visiting Galilee at Tiberias. The lake was calm. Some of the people present with him, seeing the calm, doubted whether this Bible story could be true. Almost immediately the wind sprang up, and in twenty minutes the sea was white with foam-crested waves. Great waves broke over the walls at Tiberias so that, although the visitors were 200 yards from the lake, they had to seek shelter from the blinding spray.

Matthew 8:28–34

Devils fear and fly!

Jesus, the Son of God, has authority over all spiritual powers that oppose him and his people.

Verse 28 describes the situation that Jesus faced on disembarking from the boat that had brought him and the disciples across Galilee. Two men were living in the cave-tombs in the area, and they were so violent that people feared to come near them (see also Luke 8:27–29; Mark 5:3–5). They were demon-possessed, and their condition reminds us of the power of the devil and his forces. It also shows where their power wrecks life and distorts people.

As they encounter Jesus the disciples gain an answer to their question (verse 27). They had asked, 'Who is this?' of Jesus. Now they get their answer: 'The Son of God' (verse 29 and see p. 42). The devils know that they have come face to face with their great enemy (compare James 2:19, which may have this event in mind); they know that their final destination is eternal torment (verse 29, and compare Revelation 20:3).

Verses 30–32 are very mysterious. The demons can do nothing without Jesus' permission. They ask to enter the herd of swine and the entire herd is destroyed. Why did Jesus grant the request of the demons? Possibly, it was because the time of their final judgment had not arrived. Perhaps, more likely, Jesus knew that it would teach a lesson that the inhabitants of the area needed to know. Two men had been saved from the devil's clutches. This fact was more important than anything else.

However, the owners were informed of what had happened and they forced Jesus to leave the area (verse 34). They did not bring their sick to Jesus, nor ask for the forgiveness of sins (compare 9:1–8). They were only concerned about their pigs.

This is an important point in the gospel of Matthew. He has

been describing different people's reactions to Jesus. In verses 18–22 we read about people who were almost disciples. In verses 23–27 we are told about weak disciples. Here we read about those who were faced with the truth of Jesus' identity by both words and a mighty miracle. This brought them face to face with a question: 'What is the most important thing in life?' However, rather than come to Jesus for forgiveness so that they might be God's children, they were more interested in their material possessions and their selfish ambitions. Notice that this area was mainly Gentile, so the keeping of pigs was not unlawful for these people (as it would have been for Jews). The question is more about life's priorities than about religious scruples.

Questions

1. Do you consider that your confidence in Jesus can bring you through even demonically inspired trials? What evidence can you offer? How would you recognize Satan's activity?
2. Where do you think the devil attacks church life today? Is his work more effective where he remains hidden or where he comes into the open?
3. In what way do you think that the devil is active in the world today? How does he disguise his work? If someone behaves very oddly, how can we know whether a doctor is needed, or a counsellor, or prayer for deliverance from Satan?

Where, and how many?

There are two major difficulties in connection with this story. First, the Greek manuscripts from which our Bibles are translated seem uncertain exactly where Jesus went. In Matthew's gospel the best evidence supports the word 'Gadara'. In Luke and Mark the best evidence supports 'Gerasa'.

Gergesa is also another possibility. Gerasa is 30 miles from the lake of Galilee on the south-east side. It is an unlikely place for this miracle to have taken place but its name may have been given to the entire district. Chersa (which is equivalent to Gergesa) is a suitable location and may have been a village of Gadara which was a little inland from the Sea of Galilee. Probably early copying by hand of the gospels led to this confusion.

Second, a minor problem arises because Mark and Luke only mention one man. Matthew mentions two. Probably Mark only mentioned one because he wanted to highlight the confession of the demons and the missionary commission to one of the men (Mark 5:7, 18–20) as does Luke. Matthew, however, records the full facts.

Demonic activity

This passage emphasizes the reality of demonic activity and also that such activity (scarcely if ever mentioned in the Old Testament and less in the latter part of the New Testament) occurred more regularly during the earthly ministry of Jesus. The devil and his forces were being brought face to face with their great enemy. There is no suggestion that possession is to be identified with particular sicknesses (especially mental illness). Jesus is revealed as sovereign over all the powers of darkness.

Matthew 9:1–13

Forgiveness available for all

Jesus demonstrates by another miracle that he can forgive sins and that none are excluded.

The miracle recorded in these verses is the last in the second set of three miracle stories told by Matthew. In 8:23–27 Jesus was shown to have authority over creation; in 8:28–34 he had authority over the invisible world of the spirits; now in 9:1–8 Jesus shows how he has authority to forgive sins. According to the Bible, this is something that only God can do (Psalm 103:12; Isaiah 1:18; 43:25; 55:6–7; Jeremiah 31:34; Micah 7:19). Not surprisingly, Matthew, whose great interest is the forgiveness of sins (1:21), puts this story here to emphasize that Jesus is 'the Son of God' (8:29).

Take up your mat! (verses 1–8)

With this miracle, a new stage in Jesus' ministry began. Until this point he could have been seen as merely a teacher and a miracle-worker, but now the full implications of who he claimed to be began to appear. The teachers of the law and the Pharisees were faced with a forked road. Sadly, they took the wrong path and, rather than accept Jesus' claims, they rejected him. So the opposition which led Jesus to the cross began with this healing; in the coming verses Jesus is charged with blasphemy (verses 1–8), immorality (9–13), impiety (14–17) and with being a friend of the devil (31–34). These charges will eventually bring about his death.

In 8:17 we saw that illness is sometimes the result of personal sin. The man described here seems to have believed that this was true of his paralysis. His friends, however, made great efforts to get to Jesus, taking away part of the roof canvas to let their sick friend down on a bed-roll. Jesus responded first to the man's deepest need of forgiveness by tenderly ('son', verse 2) assuring the man of his forgiveness. He may also have intended to teach the man that he was now a child of God.

The teachers of the law and Pharisees knew that only God could forgive sin. Correctly, they realized that Jesus was claiming to be God. However, without a moment's thought that Jesus might be speaking the truth, they foolishly adopted the only other possible explanation and accused Jesus of blasphemy. Jesus rebuked their false and wicked conclusion and exposed their folly. Jesus' question in verse 5 means this: 'Is it easier to claim God's power over disease and exercise it, or to assure someone of the forgiveness of sins?' The teachers would have answered that the former was more difficult. Jesus healed the man by a mere word, and he was instantly made completely fit and well (compare 8:15).

The response of the unprejudiced observers is recorded by Matthew in verse 8. The people knew they had seen a mighty display of God's power, and gave God praise for his intervention.

The call of Matthew (verses 9–13)

At the close of the second series of miracle stories (8:23 – 9:8), Matthew made it clear that Jesus has come to forgive sins. However, this fact must surely have led to two other questions: 'Who can obtain Jesus' forgiveness, and how?' In these five verses, and in a very personal way, Matthew reveals how he had discovered the answer to this question. He records his own call to discipleship, and a feast which he made for his friends to meet Jesus (see also Mark 2:13–17; Luke 5:27–32).

Matthew was a 'tax-collector'. The main trade route from Syria to Egypt went through Galilee, and Capernaum acted as a tax station as goods passed out of the territory of the tetrarch Philip into that of Herod Antipas. Matthew was apparently one of the tax officials working for Herod. These tax officials were very unpopular with the Jews; often they were extortioners, making themselves rich by taking too much money from their fellow Jews. They were also hated because they were working for the people who had conquered Palestine, and disliked because they ignored the Jewish laws. This explains why the Pharisees called them 'sinners' (verse 11). This did not necessarily mean that they despised God's law, but it did mean that they did not follow the Pharisees' understanding of it. However, many of the tax men did have a complete disregard for God.

After Jesus and his disciples had attended Matthew's feast, the Pharisees accused Jesus of impiety (see 9:1–8). Since the Pharisees believed that to have contact with bad people defiled them, how could Jesus have a meal with such people? Jesus, overhearing these remarks, gives his answer and shows the Pharisees that they had made two mistakes. They had not understood the work of the Messiah correctly, and they had falsely thought righteousness was only outward and ceremonial (see 5:17 – 6:18).

In answer to the Pharisees' mistake, Jesus told them:

- He had come as a doctor. A doctor is concerned for sick and needy people and he had come to help sinners. The Pharisees thought they were all right, but they showed no interest in those who had needs. Jesus implies that the Pharisees had been neglecting their duty.
- He used one of the religious leaders' phrases, 'Go and learn what it means', and turned it against them. He quoted Hosea 6:6, that true religion must also be accompanied by spiritual attitudes. Sadly, the Pharisees had completely misunderstood this basic Old Testament truth.

Jesus' final words were meant to be a challenge. It is not those who consider themselves good, but rather those who are in desperate need, to whom the invitation to salvation is given. He came to help the hopeless and the helpless.

Questions

1. How can you be sure that your sins are forgiven?
2. The church is a place for sinners, not saints. What implication

does this have for the life of our churches? Do we expect too high a standard from one another?

3. The church is the only organization that exists for those who are not its members. Does Jesus' ministry here give us a pattern for our own outreach?

Matthew 9:14–17

A marriage is not a funeral!

There is no place for mourning when Jesus is present. His presence should bring joy.

In 9:9–13 we read how Jesus scandalized the Pharisees. Here he puzzled a group who were sympathetic to Jesus, the disciples of John. John, a prophet whose ministry had taken place before that of Jesus (see especially 3:13–17), had taught fasting (verse 14). Fasting was a regular feature of Old Testament worship. However, it was noticeable that Jesus did not encourage his disciples to fast. Why not?

Jesus answered the challenge with several illustrations. In ancient Palestine a just-married couple remained at home and were treated like a king and queen for a week, served by special guests known as the 'children of the bride-chamber'. The week was one of great feasting and joy; such plenty was enjoyed during that week that would probably never be enjoyed again during the whole of a lifetime. The Old Testament prophets looked forward to the time when the Messiah would come. They spoke about the Messiah as a bridegroom (see Isaiah 54:5–6; 62:4–5), and the Jews had also used the picture of a wedding in connection with the coming Messiah.

Jesus' answer to John's disciples draws upon all these beliefs. He is claiming to be the Messiah who has begun to introduce the messianic age. The fasts that were appropriate before he had come were no longer appropriate (verse 15).

Two further illustrations are offered (verses 16–17). The first is of new, unshrunken material, which is added to an old much-washed garment. When the garment is washed, the original tear becomes worse. The second picture draws upon wine-making. In Palestine new wine was put in new leather skins. The skins were still soft, and were pliable when fermentation took place. Old skins could not do this; they would split.

Jesus seems to be comparing the old system of ceremonies in the Old Testament with the new age which he had introduced. The good news of Jesus and the life and power it brought could not be contained in the old rigid framework. The Old Testament ceremonies were provisional. They were appointed until Jesus would come and introduce the messianic age. The life and power of the new age made them unnecessary.

Jesus appears to be abolishing the Jewish fasts. However (compare verse 15 and 6:16–18), Jesus does not deny that voluntary fasting by individuals may still take place (see also Acts 13:2). Fasting may demonstrate that we mean business with God, may help us to show that we are not reliant on food alone for our lives and, above all, help us to focus our prayer more effectively.

Questions

1. To what extent does your faith give you great joy? Are there areas of your Christian life that cause you anxiety or stress? How can these be turned to joy? Look at James 1:2–4.
2. What place ought celebration to have in the life of the church? How is it best expressed?
3. How can we best witness our joy to a sad world?

Matthew 9:18–26

'O Death, where is your sting?'

Jesus heals the half-dead and raises the dead; here is one who has conquered death.

A third series of three miracle stories begins here. In verses 18–26 there is the double healing of Jairus's daughter and the woman with the issue of blood; in 27–31 Matthew tells us about the healing of two blind men; and in 32–34 we read the story of the exorcism of the dumb demoniac. These miracles help us to understand the nature of Jesus' kingdom. Perhaps Isaiah 35:4–6 influenced Matthew to include these stories. Sickness and death were seen there to symbolize the condition of men and women outside God's kingdom. Salvation or wholeness was to be a part of God's kingdom.

A 'ruler' or 'elder' came to Jesus. A Jewish synagogue was ruled by a board of elders, who were responsible for its day-to-day running (and the maintenance of order in the meetings). Usually such persons seem to have been enemies of Jesus. However, Jairus (Luke 8:41) was either a secret disciple or driven by his extreme circumstances to seek Jesus' help. It is more likely that he was a secret disciple, because he came and 'worshipped' Jesus (see 2:11), and because his faith is seen in his belief that, even after the death of his daughter, Jesus could bring her again to life. This is the first time a resurrection miracle is recorded.

Jesus' response to Jairus was immediate (verse 19). However, while he was on the way to Jairus's home, a very sick woman, who had suffered either a continuous or periodic issue of blood for twelve years, came to Jesus. In the Old Testament, blood was regarded as the source of life. Ritually, the woman would have been viewed as 'unclean', like the leper. This probably explains her secrecy.

The woman seems to have thought that Jesus' power was a sort of magic and that she could be healed by a touch without his knowledge. Nevertheless, Jesus met her in her need, and then told her it was faith, not magic, that had cured her (verse 22). As with the man described in verses 1–9, this woman seems to have been made conscious of her sin through her illness. So Jesus uses the word 'saved' (although the New International Version translates it 'healed') when addressing her, and reassures her by calling her 'daughter' (compare 9:2), and with such comforting words he healed her. Her healing was complete.

Jesus emphasized her faith for three reasons.

- To reward her for her belief that he would cure her instantly and completely.
- To stress that it was his personal response to her personal faith in him that cured her.
- To encourage her to seek complete reinstatement in the religious life and fellowship of God's people.

Jesus then proceeded to Jairus's house and the usual noise of an ancient Palestinian funeral (verse 23). Jesus brought this to an end with the words, 'The girl is not dead but asleep'. His words were not literally true, but then Jesus did not always intend his words to be understood literally any more than we do (see John 2:20–21; 3:3–4; 4:14–15, 32–33 and many others)! Perhaps Jesus was emphasizing that death would not 'win' in this little girl's case. Despite the attempt of the mourners to humiliate Jesus (verse 24), he did raise the little girl to life. We have already seen that only God could raise the dead. No wonder the news spread.

For Matthew, sickness and death were the result of sin entering the world (Genesis 3:16–19). The prophets had looked forward to the time when these things would be banished and men and women would be saved to enjoy God's new heaven and earth (compare Revelation 21:1–4 in the New Testament). We still wait for this to happen, but Jesus showed that he has the power that will one day fulfil all these hopes.

Questions

1. Can you think of any religious activities which you tend to regard as 'magical'? (Magic tries to manipulate mysterious forces.) Is your prayer quite free from magical overtones? Are you *totally* unsuperstitious?
2. Is faith confidence in Jesus' ability, or assurance that something we pray for will happen? Think of examples and experiences to discuss.
3. How far is it true that signs, wonders, healings, even resurrections, will convince an unbelieving world of God's presence? Should we expect such things? Consider specific examples.

Matthew 9:27–38

Unparalleled marvels!

In the place where God was used to doing miraculous things, Jesus surpassed all that had gone before. His motive was love, not display.

The miracles in 8:1–17 were acted parables of Jesus' work, those in 8:23 – 9:8 taught who Jesus really was, and in 9:18–26 Jesus' salvation was seen to include a reversal of God's curse for sin. Verses 27–34 teach that Jesus is 'great David's greater son'.

Two blind men (verses 27–34)

The Jews correctly understood that 2 Samuel 7 promised a great king who would reign for ever and spoke about a coming 'son of David'. These two blind men had heard enough about Jesus to be sure that Jesus was the promised king, even though they had seen nothing that he had done (verse 7). Jesus, typically, tried their faith; first by appearing to ignore them, and then by a test which drew out not just faith but faith in *himself*. When that faith was shown, he healed the two men by his word (verse 30). Jesus' strong desire for secrecy probably arose from his desire not to gain a following as a mere magical wonder-worker (verse 31). The men were wrong to disobey him, but their reaction is entirely understandable.

A final miracle is recounted briefly in 9:32–34. A dumb demoniac was completely healed.

To Matthew, the importance of these events lay in the double reaction described in verses 33 and 34. The crowd as a whole were amazed and said: 'Nothing like this has ever been seen in Israel.' The land of Israel was the place where God was to show his glory to the world, yet nothing like this had happened before, not even in the time of great David! No healings of blindness are recorded in the Old Testament (nor in the New Testament, apart from Jesus' miracles; Paul's experience on the Damascus road was a rather different case). Yet such healings were expected when the Messiah came. The people's hopes were beginning to come to pass before their very eyes!

Sadly, we read about another reaction (verse 34). The Pharisees couldn't deny the facts (compare Acts 4:16), but they resisted the proper interpretation. They knew Isaiah 35:3–5 and could see the promised events taking place before them, but they wouldn't believe it. What was happening did not fit in with what they thought God ought to do or what they wanted him to do.

Jesus, the tender-hearted (verses 35–38)

These verses begin a new section in Matthew's gospel (9:35 – 10:42) on the theme of discipleship. There were three elements in Jesus' ministry: teaching, preaching and healing (verse 35, see also 4:23). The first two refer to the ministry of words; the last was the word backed by deeds.

When Jesus saw the needs of the many people who came to

him, he had 'compassion' on them. His compassion was aroused by a number of things; the world's pain (Matthew 14:14; 20:34; Mark 9:22), sorrow (Luke 7:13), hunger (Matthew 15:32) and loneliness (Mark 1:41). Here, Jesus had pity upon the crowds especially because they were 'harassed and helpless' (36). The word for this in the Greek can mean skinned, completely worn out, exhausted, scattered, thrown about or lying down in an utterly helpless and forsaken condition. Jesus was moved by the crowd because he recognized them to be bewildered, exhausted and neglected by those who should have been caring for them; he seems to have been particularly concerned for their spiritual needs.

He was also aroused because of the urgency and greatness of the needs and the lack of resources (verse 37). Jesus describes a vast, ripened field of corn or wheat which requires both immediate action, or else it will be destroyed, and a large number of workers to finish it. Jesus' grief was aroused by seeing the crowd as such a field with very few to work among them. So he gave his disciples an important task to do (verse 38); he told them to pray. Why did Jesus do this? Probably because there are no excuses for prayerlessness, and because only God is able to give the necessary desires in the hearts of men and women to drive them into the harvest-field. Above all, prayer is the best way to arouse our own compassion and prepare ourselves for God's call.

Questions

1. What are the lessons to be learnt from the miracle stories of Jesus?
2. How can you improve your knowledge of the 'harvest field' and pray more effectively for it?
3. How might we ensure that 'compassion' is the first word that non-Christians use to describe the church? Is it realistic to expect?

Matthew 10:1–4

Foundation stones

Jesus chooses the band of followers who will be the foundation upon which the church is built.

In this chapter, 'the Twelve' are called and commissioned. These men had already been set aside by Jesus as a special group (Mark 3:13–19; Luke 6:12–16) but, now that they had spent time with him, they are ready to begin their unique calling (compare verses 5–15 with Mark 6:7–13; Luke 9:1–6). Matthew now describes them for the first time as 'apostles'.

Verses 2–4 provide one of the four lists of Jesus' apostles found in the New Testament (compare Mark 3:16–19; Luke 6:14–16; Acts 1:13). The names of Simon, Andrew, James, John, Philip, Bartholomew, Thomas, Matthew, James the son of Alphaeus, Simon the Zealot (or Canaanite) and Judas Iscariot are found in all the lists. Judas's name is not in Acts 1:13 because he was dead and had been removed from office. The last apostle is called Thaddaeus in Matthew and Mark (though in Matthew the original Greek has 'Lebbaeus, whose surname is Thaddaeus'), and in Luke and Acts he is called Jude the son of James. This probably means that this particular man had a number of names. This was a common practice in Bible times (and, of course, we often have several names and 'nicknames'). It is quite likely that Bartholomew was the Nathanael mentioned in John's gospel (John 1:45–51).

The people whom Jesus specially called and who would later turn the world upside-down were an ordinary but very mixed 'bunch'. Yet despite their deep differences they were united by their love for Jesus, having shared a common call.

The disciples were people like us, with both strengths and weaknesses. Yet they were all used by Jesus.

- *Peter* was the natural leader; a colourful man, full of zeal but often very unstable. He pretended to be brave, but often he was frightened inside, and yet Jesus transformed him into 'a rock'. He became the leader of the early church.

- *Andrew* was Peter's brother, one of the many people who were waiting for God's promises to be fulfilled. When Jesus first appeared, Andrew joined him (John 1:37), and it was he who brought Peter to Jesus; yet he was always happy to remain in the background (John 1:40–42). It was Andrew's home where Jesus lived in Capernaum (Mark 1:29). Andrew was a friendly man, even with children (John 12:22; 6:8–9). He was a man with weak faith, but a faith which the Lord Jesus was able to build up (John 6:8–9).

- *James* and *John* were brothers, and fishermen. They probably had a high-ranking relative because John was known to the high priest (John 18:16). They were emotional men and could get very angry (Mark 3:17) and over-zealous for Jesus (Luke 9:54–56). John was also a thoughtful man and Jesus found him to be a special friend (John 13:23; 19:26; 20:2; 21:7, 20). James was the first Christian martyr (Acts 12:2), and John was probably the last of the apostles to die (John 21:22–24).

- *Philip* came from Bethsaida (and was therefore a fellow townsman of Peter and Andrew – see John 1:44). Philip was happy to remain in the shadows. He does not seem to have been a great thinker (John 1:45–51) and he sometimes found it difficult to follow all that Jesus said (John 14:8). However, like Andrew, he was willing to learn (John 6:5–7) and was a friendly man (John 12:21–22).

- All we know about *Bartholomew* is recorded in John 1:45–49 and 21:2 (if we assume that Bartholomew and Nathanael are the same person). Bartholomew is seen to be a devout Bible student. He was inclined to have doubts. However, when the truth was revealed to him he could grasp it firmly.

- *Thomas* is mentioned in John 11:16; 14:5; 20:24–28; 21:2. He was inclined to get despondent, but he was also very devoted to his friends. Thomas was a doubter like Nathanael, but he too could be led to profound understanding of truth.
- *Matthew* was the tax-collector who left everything for Jesus (Luke 5:27–32). He was modest and humble, and in his own gospel he tells us little about himself. He is never recorded as speaking in any of the gospels. He was probably the most educated of all the disciples and zealous for his friends (Luke 5:29).
- Of the others, *Simon* was probably a brave patriot. *James* and *Thaddaeus* were less in the limelight. Finally, *Judas Iscariot* was the man who did not profit from his friendship with Jesus, nor from his experience of the things of God.

Questions

1. What encouragement can I gain from the list of people Jesus chose as his disciples? What strengths and weaknesses do I share with them?
2. Should our churches choose leaders on the same basis as Jesus? If not, why not? Is 'democratic' voting helpful? Or is it helpful to accept all who offer?
3. Are the qualifications for Christian leadership different from the leadership qualities needed, for instance, by a secular politician or the manager of a business? How?

'Apostles'

In the New Testament, the word 'apostle' is used of a large number of people. It is sometimes used of 'the Twelve', as it is here. It is also used of Matthias in Acts 1:26, often of Paul, and sometimes of other people: Barnabas (Acts 14:14), James, the Lord's brother (Galatians 1:19; 1 Corinthians 15:7), possibly Andronicus and Junias (Romans 16:7), and church envoys (2 Corinthians 8:23; Philippians 2:25).

However, 'the Twelve' do seem to occupy a special position in the New Testament (see Acts 1:26; 1 Corinthians 15:7; Revelation 21:14). Paul was later included with them.

With the exception of Paul, who recognized he was the last of the 'apostles' (1 Corinthians 15:8), all these men knew the whole course of Jesus' ministry (Acts 1:21–22), had been witnesses to his resurrection (Acts 1:22), and had received a direct call from God (Romans 1:1). They were called to preach (Mark 3:14) and to exercise in a unique way the authority of Jesus (compare Matthew 10:1 with 7:23 and 9:6). They did acts of healing and remarkable signs (2 Corinthians 12:12). After they had died, these things were called 'attesting signs'. These men were also uniquely given an understanding of God's word (Acts 2:42; John 15:26–27; 14:26). The words that they wrote down were called 'scripture' (2 Peter 3:15–16) just like the Old Testament. They form the core of our New Testament.

Matthew 10:5–15

Jesus doesn't want mercenaries

Jesus sent out the Twelve so as to extend the scope of the work that he was doing himself.

The remainder of chapter 10 describes Jesus' commission to the Twelve. It can be divided into three parts. First, verses 5–15 refer to the task that Jesus gave the Twelve on this occasion. Then, verses 16–25 look beyond their present mission to their work among the Gentiles after Jesus' death and resurrection. Finally, verses 26–42 give some general teaching on discipleship for all God's disciples in every age.

Verse 5 shows that the mission described here is a special one (compare Matthew 28:18–20) to Galilee. There were probably two reasons for this mission: the Jews had a special place in God's dealing with mankind, and their history was intended to give them the first opportunity to accept Jesus and to bring God's news to the nations (compare Romans 1:16; 2:9–10; Acts 13:46). Secondly, the disciples were not yet ready to preach to non-Jewish people.

The 'lost sheep of the house of Israel' may refer to a special group of Jews, but probably it refers to all of Israel and it would seem to look back to both 9:36 and Ezekiel 34.

The message that the Twelve were to preach was the same as that of John and Jesus (see 3:2; 4:17). They were also expected to do two of the three things that Jesus did: preaching and healing (see 4:23; 9:35). In a special, unique way they were to represent Jesus (see 10:1–2).

The commands of verses 8–10 probably reflect the practice of the Jews at the time. The disciples of Jewish teachers seemed to have lived in the same way. The instructions are probably intended to show that the disciples, by their attitude to material things, were first of all interested in the things of God; the words 'freely you have received, freely give' emphasize this. A person who possesses a precious secret should not keep it to himself or demand payment but freely pass it on. The disciples were, therefore, encouraged to put their entire trust in God. Jesus' words were also intended to arouse the responsibility of those who benefited from their work (verse 10; compare Deuteronomy 25:4; 1 Corinthians 9:7–14; 1 Timothy 5:8).

Some of Jesus' teaching here was only intended to apply to this particular mission. However, there are a number of lasting principles; a 'full-time' worker must not be over-concerned for material things, but God's people must make sure that workers get enough to meet their needs.

Verses 11–15 reflect the times in which Jesus lived. Ancient Israel did not have many inns or hotels, and travel was not easy. Hospitality to strangers was important (compare Matthew 9:10; Luke 5:29; 19:5, 10; John 12:1–2; Acts 16:14–15; 18:26; Romans

16:1–2; Philemon 7, 22; 2 Timothy 1:16; 3 John 8). It remains a mark of a true disciple (Romans 12:13; 1 Timothy 3:2; 5:10; Titus 1:8; Hebrews 13:2).

The disciples were to avoid places which might hinder their usefulness, and remain in one place in each town. They were not to give the impression that they were motivated by money, possessions or comforts.

In Palestine a greeting was offered to every home on entry and the disciples were to follow the same practice. However, they would not always be welcome. It was the custom of Pharisees when returning to Judea from a foreign land to shake the dust off their feet, to show that they wanted nothing to do with the ungodly Gentiles. The Jews who refused to believe the disciples' message were to be treated as though they were Gentiles. They no longer had any right to the blessings of God's kingdom, but were under judgment (15) – a judgment all the greater because of their greater privilege.

Questions

1. What are the things that threaten your wholehearted obedience to Jesus?
2. What implications do you think this passage has for people and countries who have had the privilege of hearing the gospel?
3. What strategy for mission should we be using today?

Matthew 10:16–25

Jesus wants battlers

Jesus here describes the hardship which will follow true discipleship.

Jesus assumes that hardship is inevitable for the true disciple. This is not the normal way to win followers, but Jesus was never interested in getting 'cheap' disciples. He wanted people who would face every opposition and battle on for him. As God's sheep (9:36) they are in constant danger, since the enemy are like wolves, ready to fall upon the sheep and violently tear them limb from limb (verse 17).

Three different 'wolf packs'

- *False religion* (especially false Christianity) has always been intolerant of the true religion of Jesus. In particular, however, Jesus speaks of the local synagogues and the regional councils of the Jews (verse 17). This was the immediate problem that the disciples would face, as the book of Acts demonstrates.
- *The state.* Jesus mentions Roman governors and the local kings who supported the Roman state (verse 18). But again his words are more widely true. The state often wants to bind people's consciences and it hates those who claim a greater authority. In the Old Testament the prophets were always in danger because they declared God's words to kings and rulers.
- *The family.* Even here opposition will sometimes not stop short of murder (verse 21). It is often in the family that the gulf between Jesus' followers and those enslaved to the devil is seen most clearly.

In some form or another, all true disciples have some experience of what Jesus teaches here (verse 22); if the world of unbelief often hates Jesus, it will often hate his representatives (verses 24–25).

How then are Jesus' disciples to face all these difficulties? Jesus offers an illustration by way of an answer (verse 16). Among the Jews, the serpent or snake was a symbol of shrewdness; the disciples were to be careful, observant and wise in all their dealings, not too trusting nor unduly provocative, careful of unbelievers' traps, and zealous to avoid doing anything that would lead to unnecessary criticism. They were also to be 'as innocent as doves' (Jesus is again drawing upon a popular illustration among the Jews here).

Jesus makes one final and very important point. No disciple is to make a martyr of himself (verse 23). Courage does not demand foolishness.

Jesus promises help (verses 19–20), even if he does not promise deliverance or a lightening of the burden. It was not humiliation or pain which the early Christians feared, but lack of speaking skills which might injure rather than commend faith in Jesus. Jesus promises that when someone is on trial for his faith, he will give words to him. The true disciple will share Jesus' sufferings before he shares his glory. Jesus refuses the fruits of victory to those who have avoided the battle.

Questions

1. Do you experience opposition as a Christian? In what ways do these verses encourage you? What is the difference between suffering because you are a Christian and enduring suffering in a Christian way?
2. Does your church seem like an army of volunteers – ready to run away at the first difficulty? If so, what might be done to solve the problem?
3. Where do Christians suffer the threat of martyrdom today? Turn your answers into prayer for them.

Matthew 10:26–42

Encouragement to faithful witnesses

Jesus offers incentives to encourage faithful discipleship and calls for wholehearted obedience.

Jesus was always realistic. He knew that sparrows did sometimes die (verse 29), and that the same fate would sometimes fall upon his followers (verse 28). He never said this didn't matter. However, he did offer a way of viewing hardship which would help remove paralysing fear. Such fear, unchecked, could lead to desertion of and rejection by Jesus.

There are six encouragements to faithful witness in these verses.

- Jesus teaches that the final recognition by God of his children ought to be an incentive to faithfulness (verses 26–27). Thus Jesus' disciples are not to be afraid to witness boldly. In ancient Palestine, the rooftop was the usual place from which public announcements were made.
- Sometimes a disciple will endanger his or her life by speaking out (verse 28). However, it is better, Jesus says, to suffer the loss of life on earth than suffer God's judgment in hell. The Bible teaches that man is a body and a soul, and the two together make up the real person. Through sin the two become separated temporarily at death but they will be reunited at the end of the present age. Death to the body is, therefore, not the final disaster that can happen to a man or a woman. Rather, the greater disaster is God's judgment.
- Nothing is ever outside God's will (verse 29; compare Romans 8:29–39). In ancient Palestine, small birds were sold very cheaply: two for a penny, or five for twopence (Luke 12:6). Yet every moment of their lives these little

birds were under God's care. If this is so, God's disciples must always be lovingly cared for by him. This does not mean that they will not suffer – even die – but it does mean that nothing happens that is not for God's glory and his people's lasting blessing.

- A very special care and love is bestowed upon God's children (verses 30–31). If God, therefore, appoints a hard path, it is a path of abounding love. This may not make things easy but it does make them bearable.
- Loyalty to Jesus will certainly be rewarded (verses 32–33). If a man is loyal to Jesus Christ in this life, Jesus will be loyal to him in the life to come.
- Nothing done for Jesus or for any of his followers goes unrewarded (verses 40–42). However great or small the disciple may be, if he is welcomed then the person who welcomes him will be rewarded.

Such wholehearted discipleship is absolutely essential. Jesus pictures only two alternatives. It is discipleship or nothing.

Questions

1. How should I apply the lessons of this section to my own life? Consider them slowly one by one.
2. Does my church place as much value on the humble as on the great disciple? If not, why not? How does this work out in practical terms?
3. Share examples in which Christians have stood up for Jesus against the opposition of the world. What was the effect of their witness?

Matthew 11:1–6

Doubts and fears

Jesus deals with the doubts of John the baptizer, who couldn't understand why Jesus wasn't doing the things he expected the Messiah to do.

These verses begin a new section in this gospel. In the next two chapters there is a great deal of teaching about faith and unbelief. We are told that Jesus is the Christ (11:2) who has come after Elijah (11:13); he is the Son of Man (11:19; 12:8–32, 40), the Servant of the Lord (12:18), the Son of David (12:23), the one on whom the Spirit of God rests (12:18, 28, 32), whose miracles are signs of the coming of the kingdom (11:20; 12:28).

However, God has hidden these things from those who do not believe, spoken of as 'this generation' (11:16; 12:39, 41, 42, 45), 'the wise and learned' (11:25), 'the Pharisees and teachers of the law' (12:2, 14, 24, 38), Jesus' 'mother and brothers' (12:46). On the other hand, God has revealed these things to 'the poor' (11:5), to those who take no offence at him (11:6), to those who have ears to hear (11:15), to 'babes' (11:25, AV), to those to whom God chooses to reveal them (11:26), who 'are weary and burdened' (11:28), the Gentiles (12:18–21), his disciples (12:49), and 'whoever does the will of my father' (12:50).

This section is a major turning-point in Matthew's gospel. The kingdom has been announced to Israel by John the Baptist (chapter 3), and by the words (chapters 5–7) and deeds (chapters 8 and 9) of Jesus, and of his apostles (chapter 10). But 'Israel' rejects the gospel (as this section begins to illustrate because of unbelief and takes offence at Jesus. As a result the way begins to open up for salvation to be preached to 'the Gentiles'. In this way Isaiah's prophecy is fulfilled in Jesus (12:18–21).

Verse 1 links chapters 10 and 11, since it was the report of

Jesus' actions that provoked John's question. John was in prison (see 4:12) where he was, apparently, allowed visitors who told him everything that Jesus was doing. When he heard the reports, John was very surprised because Jesus was not acting in the way that he had expected. He had taught that the Christ would come as a judge. This led to the question which he asked in verse 3.

Jesus did not give John a direct reply but reminded him of some Old Testament predictions which Jesus was fulfilling. In particular, Jesus seemed to have had in mind Isaiah 29:18–19; 35:5–6 and 61:1–2. He sought to show John that the miraculous acts of God, which Isaiah said would happen when the Messiah came, were actually happening in him, and the good news the prophets predicted was actually being taught by him.

Jesus was not suggesting that John had been wrong (see below on verses 7–17). Rather, John was like a man who needed spectacles. Without glasses he could not see clearly. Jesus would one day come as judge. However, before that, John needed to see that Jesus had something else to do. He had to preach the good news and die, to guarantee the things which he had taught in his gospel.

What can we learn from all this?

- The true disciple will often have doubts. Like John, we are all called to live by faith and not by sight and, because we do not see the things we hope for, we can sometimes make mistakes, expect the wrong things, and experience problems we never thought we would ever have to face. Thus faith, because it is faith, sometimes produces doubts. This is why Jesus does not criticize John, for doubt is not sin. Indeed, Jesus goes on to praise him!

- Doubt will turn to Jesus for an answer. This is what John did, and Jesus did not fail John. Jesus showed him from the scripture how he had misunderstood God's truth, and then he showed John the answer to his doubts. In the same way, our doubts should lead us to Jesus, who will give us fresh understanding from the Bible. This understanding will strengthen our faith and help to remove our doubts.

There is a very great difference between doubt and unbelief. Unbelief uses difficulties as an excuse for faithlessness, whereas doubts turn the true disciple in faith to Jesus for an answer.

Questions

1. How can this passage help me to wrestle through my doubts when I have them? In what areas do most of them lie?
2. What place does modern church life allow for the person with doubts? How can we improve the situation?
3. Jesus points John to the fulfilment of prophecy in his ministry. Do you think that this is still a good argument to use with doubters and unbelievers? What other prophecies might you point to?

Matthew 11:7–19

Faith and unbelief

Jesus emphasizes how foolish and blind people sometimes are when faced with the word of God.

In verses 7–9 Jesus reminds his hearers that they had recognized John as a prophet. They were right. John was not the sort of person who looked for favour as courtiers in a king's palace do. He both dressed and spoke like a prophet.

The Jews believed that no new prophet would arise until a new stage of God's dealings with his people was about to start. They expected one final prophet before God appeared and began to build his kingdom (Malachi 3:1 and 4:5–6). Thus, when they recognized John as a prophet, they clearly expected that

God was about to establish his kingdom.

But Jesus went on to make an even more remarkable claim. Through Malachi, God had said that 'I will send my messenger, who will prepare the way before me' (Malachi 3:1). Malachi had predicted that the final prophet would announce the appearance of God. John had been recognized by the people as the final prophet. He had pointed to Jesus, and Jesus says that this is exactly what Malachi had taught. Thus Jesus is claiming to be God, made Man! No wonder John was more than a prophet!

The Jews also expected that God would establish his kingdom when he came, but many of them misunderstood what it would be like. Jesus shows clearly that he had begun to build the predicted kingdom (verses 11–12).

The meaning of verse 12 is hotly debated. It seems that Jesus is saying that the kingdom began to appear when he started his ministry, but opposition to it has not abated. Jesus reminded his hearers that the whole of the Old Testament writings were always pointing forward; pointing to John and his message that God was about to come (verses 13–14). The evidence is now before Jesus' hearers – but are they courageous enough to recognize it (verse 15)?

In verses 16–19 Jesus describes a quite different group of people: those who *will* not believe. They have all the same evidence as those who hear (verse 15) but they do not respond in the same way. Jesus compares them to children who act childishly and will not play whatever the game is. Whatever is offered, it is never right. John and Jesus lived quite differently but were both equally rejected. However God's word came, people found fault with it; only blind prejudice could explain such behaviour.

The end of verse 19 describes the tragic result of unbelief. It simply gets nowhere. Yet in this life and the age to come John's and Jesus' message will be clearly vindicated.

Questions

1. What examples of blind unbelief have you encountered? What is the best response you can offer?

2. In what sense are ordinary church members ('least in the kingdom of heaven') 'greater' than John the Baptist, the greatest man who had ever lived (verse 11)? Is this really true or some sort of exaggeration? What are the implications for your church?
3. Why does the kingdom of God provoke such violent opposition?

John and Elijah

Jesus' statements both here and in 17:12 do not contradict John's denial that he was Elijah (John 1:21). The Jews had come to expect that Elijah would personally return to earth. John, quite rightly, denied that he was Elijah. However, the Old Testament prophets often spoke about the future by using names or events from the past. They did not speak literally. They meant that something or someone who resembled the earlier person or event would come in the future. John was a prophet like Elijah (compare Mark 1:6 with 2 Kings 1:8). Jesus understood this and taught that John 'was' the predicted Elijah.

Matthew 11:20–30

Missed opportunities and rest for the weary

Jesus bewails the fact that many hear the good news but tragically and wilfully reject it. He offers a tender invitation to all who need rest.

The tragedy of a missed opportunity (verses 20–24)

Most of Jesus' ministry of teaching and healing took place in Galilee. The towns of Korazin, Bethsaida and Capernaum were in Galilee. Indeed, Capernaum was the centre of Jesus' ministry. Tyre and Sidon were two ports on the Mediterranean Sea in what is now Lebanon, but was then Phoenicia. They were not Jewish, and the Old Testament prophets had frequently singled out these two towns as especially wicked and evil (see Isaiah 23; Ezekiel 26 – 28; Amos 1:9; Joel 3:6).

Sodom is first mentioned in Genesis 19. Later in the Old Testament it is used as an illustration of wicked men at their worst. Verse 23 is a quotation from the Old Testament. In Isaiah 14:13–14 the city of Babylon frequently symbolized the great enemy of God. Here those words are applied to Capernaum. Finally, note that 'sackcloth' (verse 21) was black in colour and was a customary garment for those in mourning. The use of ashes on the head was also a traditional sign of great grief in the ancient world.

With this knowledge we can understand Jesus' expression of real sorrow at a tragedy that is unfolding before his eyes. At the same time, perhaps he is making an emotional appeal, calculated to arouse a response in hearts that up to this time have rejected him.

The people to whom Jesus was speaking had had ample opportunity to hear Jesus, see his works and respond to him. Instead, they had almost all acted like the perverse children Jesus described in the previous verses. Despite their great privilege, they had neglected the responsibility to believe, they had been indifferent to Jesus' words and they had done nothing about the claims he made upon them. Jesus mentions especially his miracles. If his words were not enough, surely his miracles ought to have made them aware of their need for repentance. But the people had remained so stubborn that the rebellious language of Old Testament Babylon is no different from the language that they had used in rejecting Jesus. He emphasizes that the most open of sinners (Sodom) and the most vicious of men (Tyre and Sidon) would have repented if they had had the same privileges as the Galileans.

Come and welcome Jesus! (verses 25–30)

Although clever men in their wickedness cannot come to the truth about Jesus, God reveals his truth to the childlike (verses 25–26). In an older person, prejudice and clever arguments often lead to intellectual and moral blindness. Young children, however, are usually good judges of a person. Thus the 'childlike' receive when others cannot do so.

Verse 27 contains one of the most important truths in the whole Bible. Jesus had just taught that the way of salvation was by childlike response to him. He can supply what the sinner needs. Men and women need to know God. Jesus says the person who has seen him has seen God because he is the Son. There is no other way to know God which is available to men and women (John 14:6; Acts 4:12).

Verses 28–30 form wonderful climax to this chapter. They are the tender words of a merciful Saviour who wants everyone to be saved.

Jesus describes his hearers as 'weary and burdened'. Possibly he was thinking of Genesis 3:16–19, where the burdensome results of sin are described. We live in a world which is God's world – but it is flawed by sin. As a result, sorrow, sadness and mourning are never far from our experience. Jesus may also have been thinking of all those who were burdened under the heavy load of Jewish rules and laws. The Jews assumed that getting to God was difficult, so they made it very burdensome! Many religions today are just as burdensome.

To these people Jesus says 'I will give you rest'. For the Jews of Jesus' time, rest would have meant two things: life at its best and fullest, and spiritual rest (peace of mind and heart as a result of peace with God). This is the good news Jesus offers! In Jesus we may enjoy a quality of life which makes our old life a pale reflection of the real thing. With Jesus, we will one day enjoy a life free from every burden of sin (Revelation 21:1–4). Even now we can be free from all the anxieties of men and women who are trying to win God's favour. In Jesus, we can be *sure* of God's love, and we can be at peace in our minds!

How, then, is this wonderful experience to be found? Jesus asks no hard conditions; he does not ask us to *do* anything. He only asks us to *come* as we are to him and follow him. He is 'gentle and humble in heart'; very tender and merciful, especially to sinners like us. He seemed to have been thinking of Isaiah 42:3, where Isaiah paints a beautiful picture of the coming Christ. He tells us: 'a bruised reed he will not break, and a smouldering wick he will not snuff out'. The world we live in and the religions invented by men can be hard and unyielding, but not Jesus. He is a gentle Saviour.

The second encouragement that Jesus gives to his hearers is 'my yoke is easy and my burden is light'. The world and man-made religions can be harsh and their load unbearable, but obedience to Jesus is quite different. Those things we are 'to learn of him' are lightweight by comparison.

The final encouragement is a promise: 'you will find rest'. We can find rest in Christ, rest of conscience and heart, forgiveness and freedom from guilt, rest flowing from peace with God and a hope of eternal rest.

Questions

1. Is your picture of God more often that of someone with a big stick than of a loving Father? How can such ingrained images

of God be changed? What might you learn from this passage?
2. How far is your church making religion a burden for its members? Are you all carrying the church, or is the church allowing Jesus to carry you? What can you do about it?
3. 'My yoke is easy', but the Christian life is sometimes very tough and demands sacrifice (see 16:24–26). How can we understand this?

Matthew 12:1–14

Jesus fulfils the Old Testament

Jesus is greater than the greatest people in the Old Testament, the one to whom the Old Testament points.

Chapter 12 shows how the opposition of the Pharisees to Jesus developed. Here we see the first definite steps towards the cross. There are four stages: growing suspicion (verses 1–8), hostile investigation (9–13), evil opposition (14), leading to deliberate and prejudiced blindness to Jesus (22–32).

Jesus answers this challenge with courageous defiance (9–14), warning (22–23), and with a staggering series of claims; he is greater than the temple (verse 6; the temple was the most sacred place in all the world for the Jews), than Jonah (verse 41) and Solomon (verse 42). Jesus' claim is that there is nothing or no-one in spiritual history greater than he. He invites us to receive this truth.

Arguments about the Sabbath

Verses 1–14 need some explanation. In Deuteronomy 23:25 we read that God said: 'If you enter your neighbour's cornfield, you may pick the ears with your hands, but you must not put a sickle to the standing corn.'

This event took place on the Sabbath, however, and according to those same laws of God work was forbidden on the Sabbath (see Exodus 20:8–11; 34:21; Deuteronomy 5:12–15). The Pharisees believed it was necessary to define exactly what work was, so that nobody would break these laws. The disciples would have been regarded as guilty because, by plucking the ears of corn, they were reaping; by rubbing it in their hands, they were threshing; by separating the grain and the chaff, they were winnowing; and by the whole process they were preparing a meal on the Sabbath day. This explains the Pharisees' reaction in verse 2.

Jesus' reply is in two parts. In verses 3–5 he appeals to the Scriptures and shows that the Pharisees' traditions were wrong. The Bible itself teaches that it is right to set aside one of the rituals that God has appointed when human need is involved. Jesus refers to 1 Samuel 21, where the bread that had been set aside in the temple for the priests alone to eat was given to David when he was hungry. Some think that this very passage would have been read in the religious meetings of the Pharisees on the day all this happened. If so, it shows Jesus' response to the Pharisees was especially appropriate.

Then Jesus reminds his hearers that the priests were commanded to work on the Sabbath (see Leviticus 24:8–9; 1 Chronicles 9:32; 23:31). In this way, Jesus shows that in the service of God a breach of the law could take place. And the disciples were in the service of God, for they were serving the Lord on the Sabbath!

Further, the disciples were not merely serving in the temple, which symbolizes the presence of God, but were serving the God-man – someone far greater than a mere building, the one who brings the very rest that the Sabbath was intended to point to (compare verse 8 with 11:29–30).

Jesus made one other point. He quoted Hosea 6:6, a verse which taught that God is a kind God, and that kindness should be the first consideration in any action, not detailed obedience to a ritual. This showed how the Pharisees' religion had become harsh and unyielding (see 11:28–30). This is illustrated by the incident recorded in verses 9–14. They taught that only people who were in danger of dying were to be treated on the Sabbath.

This explains their question in verse 10.

In his reply (verse 11), Jesus appealed to their own rules. Even their own tradition allowed them to rescue a sheep which had an accident, whatever the day, and since people are more important than sheep (and the Pharisees would have agreed with that), it was appropriate for Jesus to heal sick people on the Sabbath. Having shown that he was right, Jesus healed the man with the withered arm (verse 13).

Sadly, the Pharisees were so inflexible and unwilling to listen even to the teaching of the Bible that they allied with their greatest enemies – the Herodians (Mark 3:6) – in order to plot Jesus' overthrow.

Questions

1. Reflect upon the claims Jesus makes for himself in this passage. What implications ought they to have for you?
2. Make a list of your church's customs, principles and ways of doing things that are really important to you all. How far would you be ready to abandon them if God made it clear that you should? (Look at Acts 10:9–16.)
3. Should we seek to 'keep Sunday special' and, if so, why? Have we any right to influence non-Christians in this matter? Why? Or, why not?

Jesus and the Sabbath

What relevance does this passage have for us? First of all, it tells us that Jesus is our 'sabbath rest'. In the Old Testament, the Sabbath was a day which looked back to the perfection of the world as it was first created, and it looked forward to the time when God would remake heaven and earth; it anticipated the delighted rest of God's people together. The New Testament teaches us that in Jesus the Sabbath has arrived. He is the 'rest' of all true disciples (Hebrews 4), and in Jesus the true disciple already has one foot in the new heaven and one on the new earth (Ephesians 1:3). Jesus is here teaching the same thing: the shadow which pointed to him must now pass away. This is why Paul in Colossians 2:16 can speak of 'Sabbaths' as shadows abolished by Jesus. For the true disciple, this means that his whole life is the enjoyment of the Sabbath rest. It is not a day but Jesus that we enjoy!

This teaching also means that Jesus, not Sunday, is our sabbath. While it is true that regular periods of work and rest are good for us and it is right to have special times when we meet together with God's people, we should never think of Sunday as a Sabbath, a day purely of 'thou shalt nots'. If we do, we are still living in the shadows. Rather, Sunday is a day for joyful celebration of all that Jesus means for us.

Matthew 12:15–21

Jesus the hope of the world

Jesus, the promised Messiah of the Old Testament, gently offers the hope of salvation to the whole world.

In 11:28–30 Jesus offered rest, in 12:1–14 Jesus showed that he is the true rest; a rest the religious leaders of the Jews rejected. Consequently, in 12:15 he left them in their darkness. However, there are those who followed him. Significantly, many of them were not Jews at all and, for Matthew who is writing the story, this seems to have been very important. The Jews rejected Jesus and the time for repentance was passing. From now on, the true people of God would be those who responded to Jesus' invitation and followed him.

In verses 18–21 Matthew quotes Isaiah 42:1–4, his longest

quotation of the Old Testament and one he clearly believed to be very important. The passage in Isaiah was understood by the Jews to point forward to the Messiah, and Matthew shows how Jesus fulfilled it. At his baptism God spoke words which echoed verse 18. Verses 19 and 20 surely describe the self-effacing tenderness with which Jesus was dealing with those who followed him (as verse 16 had already shown). Above all, verse 21 reminds us that the Messiah will be the joy of the whole earth: not just the Jews.

Questions

1. Think about Jesus' ministry-style in verses 16, 19–20. How far should we try to make a 'big splash' with the gospel, use publicity, conduct campaigns, etc.?
2. Jesus' ministry stretched out beyond the usual groups to which the kingdom was thought to belong. What implications does this have for the evangelism and mission priorities of our churches?
3. 'In his name the nations will put their hope.' But how can they, without messengers going to them? List ways in which the Good News can be shared (e.g. by people, prayer, giving, radio, the internet. . . .). Where can your group add some impetus?

Matthew 12:22–37

Growing faith and deepening unbelief

Jesus' ministry sharpens responses; some grow in their understanding of him, but others, self-blinded, sink into perverse and inescapable unbelief.

In chapters 11 and 12, the two contrasting themes of faith in Jesus and the response of unbelief have been set alongside one another. In 12:22–37 there is a climax: in verses 22–23 the response of ordinary people to Jesus is described, but in verses 24–37 that of the Pharisees.

The Jews did exorcisms (verse 27), but Jesus' word of authority effected a complete and immediate healing. This explains the amazement of those who saw what happened and led them to think about what the Old Testament taught. In Isaiah 35:5, such remarkable healings had been predicted when God established his kingdom, and the Jews had, quite rightly, expected that kingdom to be ruled by 'great David's greater Son' as Ezekiel had also predicted (35:23; 37:25). So, in response to Jesus' remarkable exorcism, the people naturally began to ask, 'Could this be the Son of David?' (verse 23). They began to grow in their understanding of Jesus, though they still had doubts because he was so unlike the picture of the Son of David which they had been brought up to expect.

A horrifying blasphemy

Verses 24–37 describe an enormous contrast. The Pharisees obstinately clung to their system of religious misunderstandings, and were forced by an undeniable miracle to the only alternative explanation. Their explanation was, however, a horrifying blasphemy (verse 24).

Jesus replied to the Pharisees by very carefully making five points: the charge is absurd (verses 25–26); inconsistent (verse 27); obscures the truth (verses 28–30); is unpardonable (verses 31–32); and shows up the wickedness of those who make the charge (verses 33–37).

- In verses 25–26, Jesus shows the Pharisees how absurd their claim is; it is ridiculous, he says, to suggest that Satan would oppose Satan. If this were so, he would be destroying his own work.
- But the Pharisees' claim is also inconsistent. If the exorcisms of the Jews were God's work, how do they suppose a greater display of power in exorcism to be Satan's. The claim of the Pharisees is thus doubly inconsistent. It claims that the Jews perform the work in one way, and Jesus in another. More seriously, the Pharisees are suggesting that the greater power is that of Satan!
- In verses 28–30, Jesus explains that the exorcism in fact shows that he has power over Satan and is able to rob him. The question of the ordinary people in verse 23 was a correct one, since Jesus has demonstrated he is able to break the power of Satan and establish God's kingdom (verse 28). It is not unlikely that Jesus had Genesis 3:15 in mind, where God had predicted that one of Adam's descendants would one day come and defeat the devil who had tempted Adam and all men into sin. Either men and women recognize this, or they are the enemies of Jesus and of God (verse 30).
- The Pharisees' attitude was unpardonable (verses 31–32). In blaspheming against Jesus, the Pharisees were not merely criticizing Jesus, but the Spirit of God who was working in him. The sin against Jesus was forgivable: Jesus was still working in a way which partly hid who he really was. However, when the Holy Spirit worked so openly, the sin was inexcusable.
- Finally (verses 33–37), Jesus shows the reason for the Pharisees' attitude was in their wickedness. They were incapable of coming to repentance.

This section teaches us two important lessons. First, if we come with open minds to Jesus, he will give us an increasing understanding of his work and who he is. However, secondly, if we don't come to Jesus, the reason is that we are in rebellion against him and do not want him. The evidence to this will be seen in the absurd reasons (which human beings perversely usually think are clever) we find not to believe. The evidence points all in one direction: only prejudice can think otherwise!

Questions

1. How can you daily ensure that you grow in your knowledge of Jesus?
2. How should we counsel those who fear they have committed the unpardonable sin (see below)?
3. How does this passage help explain the stubborn resistance to the gospel which evangelistic and mission work often encounters?

The blasphemy against the Spirit

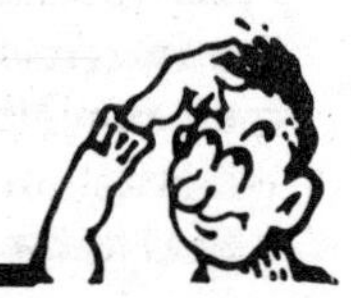

Some Christians get very concerned about whether or not they have committed the blasphemy against the Spirit. What, then, is this blasphemy against the Spirit? William Hendriksen says,

> We learn that in this passage the Pharisees were ascribing to Satan what the Holy Spirit 'through Christ' was achieving. Moreover, they were doing this wilfully and deliberately. In spite of all the evidence to the contrary they still affirmed that Jesus was expelling demons by the power of the devil. Not only this, they were making progress in sin as a comparison between 9:11 and 12:2, 4 clearly shows. Now, as has been already shown, to be forgiven implies that the sinner is truly repentant (Mark 3:28; Luke 12:10). Among the Pharisees here

described, such genuine sorrow for sin is totally lacking. For penitence they substitute hardening; for confession, plotting. Thus by means of their own criminal and completely inexcusable callousness they are dooming themselves. Their sin is unpardonable because they are unwilling to tread the path that leads to pardon. For a thief, an adulterer, and a murderer, there is hope. The message of the gospel may cause him to cry out: 'O God be merciful to me, the sinner' but when a man has become hardened so that he has made up his mind not to pay any attention to the promptings of the Holy Spirit, not ever to listen to his pleading and warning voice, he has placed himself on the road that leads to perdition. He has sinned the sin 'unto death' (1 John 5:16).

For anyone who is truly penitent no matter how shameful his transgression may have been, there is no reason to despair (Psalm 103:12; Isaiah 1:18; 44:22; 55:6, 7; Micah 7:18–20; 1 John 1:9). On the other hand there is no excuse for being indifferent as if the subject of the unpardonable sin is of no concern to the average church member. The blasphemy against the Spirit is the result of gradual progress in sin. Grieving the Spirit (Ephesians 4:30), if unrepented of, leads to resisting the Spirit (Acts 7:51), which, if persisted in, develops in quenching the Spirit (1 Thessalonians 5:19). The true solution is found in Psalm 75:78 (W. Hendrickson, *The Gospel of Matthew*, Banner of Truth, 1974, p. 575).

Matthew 12:38-50

Playing the games of unbelief

Rather than face the challenge of Jesus' ministry, the Jewish leaders resort to a 'verbal smoke screen', hiding behind clever but foolish arguments.

Resenting Jesus' reply to their charge (verse 24), the Pharisees got together with the teachers of the law, the so-called expert interpreters of the Bible, and came up with a very clever argument.

They asked not for a miracle but for a 'sign' from Jesus. In the Bible this word refers to the events which would herald the coming of God's kingdom. In particular they ask Jesus for a 'miraculous' sign. Probably by asking this they were suggesting that, since Moses (who had written their law) had been shown to be God's prophet by thunder and lightning and manna from heaven, the greater prophet of which Moses spoke would have the same sort of signs.

Because the Pharisees were asking their question out of unbelief, Jesus refused to give them a sign. In the Old Testament God's relationship with his people was described as a marriage. When that relationship was broken it was, therefore, commonly described as adultery. Jesus taught that the teachers of the law doubted him because they had departed from God. Sensitive students of the Old Testament would have come to the right conclusions in the light of Jesus' work and ministry. Since this was so, a sign would be pointless, because even that would not change the minds of the Pharisees.

Jesus explained his point more fully (verses 41–42) by contrasting first the Ninevites of Jonah's day and then the Queen of Sheba (see 1 Kings 10:1–13) with the Pharisees. The Ninevites, without any spiritual advantages, repented at the preaching of a minor prophet who performed no miracles and was a rebellious, stupid man. Moreover, the Queen of Sheba came from a great distance to meet Solomon, and responded to his wisdom. However, the teachers of the law and the Pharisees, with far greater advantages and far more evidence, were rejecting Jesus and plotting against him.

Thus, extra evidence would be of no value. One great sign would be given, his resurrection (hinted at in verses 39 and 40), but even this would not persuade his enemies (see Luke 16:19–31).

Warning and encouragement

Jesus goes on to emphasize the dangerous condition of those who refuse to welcome him, but shows that he will cheerfully welcome all those who follow him. Verses 43–45 are probably best understood in the light of Jewish history. Before the exile in Babylon, the Jewish people had been guilty of the worst forms of idol worship, and the exile was God's judgment on them. The result was that the people who returned to Palestine rejected all idolatry. However, by Jesus' time they had developed a religion that was even worse: for it couldn't recognize Jesus when he appeared.

Jesus' parable points to the tragedy of their situation. Satan was now their master even more than he had been before. Possibly there is also a reference here to John the Baptist. Many had responded to John's preaching but, when Jesus had appeared, they had failed to understand that John had pointed to Jesus and they were now opposing Jesus.

Members of Jesus' family then visit him (verses 46–50; see Mark 3:21–22 for the background). Jesus uses this to illustrate an important point to his hearers. The true children of God are the disciples, the true believers, who follow him.

Questions

1. What clever but foolish arguments have your friends used to explain why they are not Christians? How do you respond to them?

2. Why do so many professing Christians fall away from the faith?
3. Do you think that a whole 'generation' – a country, tribe or group – can become evil and adulterous, hardened in sin and resistant to God? What are the implications of this for mission?

Matthew 13:1–9

Listening to Jesus

The well-known parable of the sower is told by Jesus to encourage his hearers to receive his teaching.

Matthew now introduces an extended account of Jesus' parables. So far Jesus' teaching has included some elements of parable (see 5:13; 6:26–30; 7:24–27; 9:16–17; 11:16–17), but from this point the parables are fully developed and vivid, and will be the main vehicle for his teaching.

Another important change takes place in Jesus' ministry at this point. The religious rulers of the day had come to their final conclusion about Jesus: he was from the devil (12:24). Jesus recognized that this made it impossible for them ever to receive him (12:31–32). The time had come to withdraw from those who stubbornly refused to follow him (12:15) and he was ready to go to those who would hear him gladly (12:16–21). This explains why Jesus exchanges the place of debate with the religious leaders (especially their meeting-houses, the synagogues) for the seashore (verse 1). He also adopts a teaching method which will benefit those who want to follow him but will make the darkness resulting from the wilful misunderstandings of his enemies blacker still (see below on verses 10–17).

When Jesus had found a suitable place from which to speak to the crowd (verse 2), he began to tell the story. Perhaps as he did so, a sower was engaged in his work on one of the surrounding hills. Certainly, Jesus' hearers would have known exactly what he was talking about.

In ancient Palestine the fields were long and thin, and between each field there was a public footpath of earth which had been trampled as hard as a concrete pavement. This is what Jesus meant by 'the wayside'. Seed was scattered by hand – so as the sower went about his work, some of the seed would naturally fall on this 'pavement'. However good the seed, it could never yield a crop when it fell there.

Most of the hilly areas of Palestine were also rocky. The soil was not very deep, and hard rock was just beneath the surface. This naturally meant that there was little water in the soil. A seed would begin to grow if it fell into such soil but then, without water to draw on, it would soon die. A good sower would not deliberately cast seed into weed beds. However, weeds always seem to grow more quickly than good seed and, without weeding, the strong weeds choke the good seed and kill it. Ploughing usually took place *after* sowing, so the growing grain had to compete with the weeds as they re-established themselves.

When the seed falls into good ground it produces a harvest. The figures that Jesus mentions for the crop may be deliberately high. Certainly in ancient Palestine a crop producing tenfold was good. However, if Jesus refers to the individual seed, not the crop, the figure is, perhaps, what might have been expected. The exact figures are not important. All spiritual growth is a cause for rejoicing.

Questions

1. In what ways do any of the kinds of ground in this parable describe you?
2. Make up another parable, set in modern times, which makes the same points as 'the sower'. How easy was it?
3. What can we learn from the sower, the seed, the soil and the harvest? How does this all help us to understand the wider world beyond the church?

Matthew 13:10–23

The parable explained

Parables are meant to confuse(!) and to clarify. This one diagnoses our spiritual fitness.

After hearing Jesus' story, the disciples asked a natural question. Why, they say, are you now using this particular way to teach your hearers (verse 10)?

Jesus' reply is given in two parts (verses 12–15 and 16–17, with a summary in verse 11). First, parables are given to further confuse the hearers! Those who persist in rebellious unbelief will find that even the little understanding that they have is confused by the stories (verse 12). The reason for this is given by Jesus in verses 14 and 15 where he quotes Isaiah 6:9–10; calloused hearts make it impossible for the hearer to receive the truth and come to repentance, and the parables of Jesus only confirm men and women in that condition. Parables, like Jesus' signs, were and are a testimony to Jesus to the open-minded person who is prepared to listen. Those who refuse to listen, however, can only be further confused by them.

The same words which condemn the unbeliever in a deeper darkness give a clearer understanding to the person who wants to follow Jesus (verses 16–17). Indeed, such a person has greater understanding than even the greatest spiritual men in the Old Testament! The prophets (for example Samuel and Isaiah) and the children of God (for example Noah and Abraham) looked forward with great longing to the coming of Jesus. What they saw, however, they saw only very dimly. Jesus' hearers who were open-minded would learn that Jesus himself was the person who fulfilled all the hopes of those who lived in Old Testament times!

Jesus first told the parable (verses 3–9), and then explained to his disciples why he was teaching in parables (verses 10–17). It only remained for him to explain how to understand them.

The seed and the ground

Jesus makes nothing of who the sower is. The important thing is that the seed is God's revelation, and the essential lesson is the effect of the seed on different hearers: hearers who are like the various types of ground. The lessons Jesus teaches are these.

- The way we receive God's revelation is all-important. There is nothing wrong with the message, nor is there anything wrong with the messenger. The problem lies with the hearer, who is here likened to different types of soil.
- Some people are unteachable. The seed sown upon the wayside could never take root, however skilful the sower and however good the seed. Men and women with closed minds, insensitive hearts, and unteachable spirits can never receive the gospel to their benefit; they may hear it but they never actually listen.
- Some people are shallow hearers. Jesus describes ground where the covering of soil over bed-rock is very thin and uses this to speak of people who do hear and listen. They find the message appealing, meeting a sense of need and they welcome it often with great enthusiasm. However, the sudden enthusiasm soon becomes a dying fire.
- Some people are pre-occupied hearers. In the case of the seed that fell among thistles there was nothing much wrong with the soil. The person described hears, receives and even acts in a Christian way for a while. The problem, however, is that powerful influences arise and overcome the Christian profession.
- Some hearers will bear fruit from listening. Their fruitfulness will vary according to their gifts but each one of them will be useful in the service of Jesus.

This passage exposes those attitudes which we often have to Jesus and his message. We naturally tend to shrink from such exposure. But we must be willing to listen to Jesus' diagnosis.

Questions

1. Do you think that Jesus' explanation of the parable of the sower is the only possible one, or is it an example of how to approach parables? Consider other possible ways of looking at it before you make up your mind.
2. Do you consider that many of the pastoral problems in the church arise from faulty hearing of the word of God? What thorns and thistles spoil our harvest?
3. In what ways today do we see people prevented from coming to full discipleship as a result of being the sort of ground described here? Is there nothing we can do about it?

Matthew 13:24–30, 36–43

Side by side

Jesus explains that, though evil people may live alongside his disciples now, this situation will not exist for ever.

Chapter 13:24–52 forms a single section of Matthew's gospel, recording a further six parables. The structure is:

- Verses 24–30 Parable of the weeds
- Verses 31–35 Two parables: mustard seed and yeast
- Verses 36–43 Interpretation of the parable of the weeds
- Verses 44–46 Two parables: hidden treasure and the pearl of great price
- Verses 47–50 Parable of the net (which has the same meaning as the parable of the weeds)

Matthew highlights the importance of the two main parables and their meaning (verses 24–30, 47–50 and 36–43).

The weeds

As with so many of Jesus' stories, the parable of the weeds draws upon the common experience of farmers in ancient Palestine. In Palestine (and especially around Hebron) there was, and is, a prolific weed called the bearded darnel. When it begins to grow, it is impossible to distinguish it from wheat, and it is only when the heads appear that it is easy to recognize. However, by that time the roots of the wheat and darnel are so intertwined that the darnel cannot be uprooted without bringing up the wheat. At harvest time, however, it is vital that they are separated, because darnel has a bitter and unpleasant taste and is slightly poisonous; a drug which causes dizziness and sickness.

An enemy might show his spite by secretly sowing darnel in a farmer's field. This sort of crime must have been frequent, since the Roman laws specifically forbade it and laid down strict punishments. In Jesus' story an enemy has been at work. In normal circumstances the question of the servants would have been natural (verse 28). However, the farmer recognizes the crop is too far developed: the weeds and wheat must grow together until the final harvest, when the weeds will be gathered up and burnt.

The meaning

When Jesus interpreted the parable he began by identifying the various parts in the story (verses 37–39), and then gave the meaning (verses 40–42).

Jesus had already taught that his kingdom would one day extend throughout the world (verses 31–35). However, the world that both we and his hearers experience is a mixture of good and bad; followers of Jesus and those who will not serve him live side by side. In Jesus' story even the angels are puzzled by this. Jesus' point is that the present state of affairs is not the final one, and wickedness will, one day, be completely removed (see Joel 3:13; Jeremiah 51:33; Hosea 6:11). Those who have not followed Jesus will be finally condemned, and his followers will then be able to enjoy his kingdom to the full (verse 43).

In verse 42 Jesus used language well known to the Jews to describe God's final judgment, and the never-ending suffering of those who had rejected God's ways. (See also Jude 6–7; Revelation 14:9–11; 20:10, etc.) The picture Jesus painted is a very solemn one, because he wanted his hearers to be sure that they had understood and responded to his warning (verse 43). Jesus does not tell us here why the wicked and his disciples will live together in this present world – but elsewhere the Bible tells us it is because God is merciful. God does not want to act in judgment. He gives time to each of us to change our mind.

Questions

1. What comfort and challenge can I take away from this passage?
2. Is it possible to live entirely separated from 'the world' as some sects have tried to? How far should we be involved with the world? Where can we draw the lines?
3. How literally do we take the vivid picture of the furnace and the gnashing of teeth? How can we warn an unbelieving world about its future destiny while our 'roots are still entwined'?

Matthew 13:31–35, 44–46

Big trees from little acorns

Though the kingdom of Jesus has a small beginning, it will have a wonderful end.

Jesus had been brought up in Galilee, and much of his work had taken place there. In Galilee there was a bush known as the mustard bush; it had a tiny seed but eventually produced large bushes about 12 to 15 feet tall which became a home for nesting birds. This lies behind Jesus' parable. Similarly, in both the ancient world and the Old Testament (see Ezekiel 31:6), one of the commonest pictures of a great, worldwide empire to which all were subject was a tree to which nesting birds flocked.

Jesus taught that he had brought God's kingdom into existence. Simply looking at this wandering teacher and healer, this must have been very difficult to believe, especially for the Jews, since their prophets had spoken of a worldwide kingdom of God.

Jesus' point, therefore, is to teach that one day God's kingdom will extend throughout the world, just as the prophets had predicted (compare Isaiah 2:2–4; 25:6–9; 35:1–10; 65:17–25). Jesus had begun to establish that kingdom, the signs were there (as Matthew's earlier use of Isaiah 35:5–6 was intended to show), and from these little beginnings the expected kingdom would grow. Jesus, one day, would (will!) reign over the whole earth.

Another parable makes a similar point (verse 33). The yeast cannot be seen when first placed in the flour, but its effects are clearly visible when baking is finished. The whole of the loaf is transformed by the yeast. The beginning of the kingdom Jesus established may be hidden from sight, but one day it will be there for all to see.

In verse 35, Matthew quotes Psalm 78, which foretold the use of parables. No teacher ever revealed more amazing things in parables than Jesus. He was the great teacher.

Priceless treasure

In the ancient world there were no banks, certainly not for ordinary people, and they used the ground to hide away their valuables because it was often the safest place (see also 5:25). Palestine was often a battle field. People would therefore hide their valuables in the ground before they fled, hoping, one day, to return and regain them. Even today, remarkable discoveries of treasures are unexpectedly made in Palestine, for example the Dead Sea Scrolls. This was a complete library of 'books' going back to the time of Jesus, which had been hidden in a cave. Perhaps some recent and similar discovery prompted Jesus' parable.

The man described in the story was probably a day labourer; he was certainly very poor if he had to sell everything to buy a field. However, to obtain this treasure, he sacrificed everything else for the field.

The second parable (verses 45–46) is very similar. In the ancient world, a pearl was the most prized possession of all. In the story a rich merchant (by comparison to the poor day-labourer of 44) finds a unique pearl. For that pearl he, too, willingly sells everything for the pleasure and enjoyment of possessing it.

In telling these two parables, Jesus repeated the same point to be sure it was grasped.

- To be in Jesus' kingdom was delightful. The day labourer went with joy to purchase the field, and the merchant sought something which would bring him great joy and admiration: a priceless treasure. Following Jesus and entering his kingdom is such a delight.
- To enter Jesus' kingdom demands our total response. Whether we are poor or wealthy, we must be willing to forsake everything in order to follow him.
- We notice that two different types of discovery are

described in these two parables. First, there is the man who makes an unexpected discovery. Secondly, we are told of a person who is diligently seeking pearls. Some unexpectedly come upon the riches of Jesus' kingdom; for others it is the end of a long search. Either way, it is a superlative experience to find and enjoy Jesus' kingdom.

Questions

1. What joys have you found in knowing Jesus? Can you trace growth from small beginnings in your life?
2. How should the church show that it possesses a rare, priceless treasure?
3. What does it mean, practically, to 'sell all that we have' in order to possess the kingdom of heaven? Or does Jesus intend us to take these words literally?

Matthew 13:47–58

Judgment awaits sinners

Jesus stresses that judgment will one day fall upon unbelievers. He is then himself judged and rejected by his own people.

The drag-net was often used in ancient Palestine. This was a large square net with ropes at each corner. It was weighted so that when at rest in the water it hung upright. However, when the boat began to move, the net was drawn into a large cone into which the fish were swept. This form of fishing meant that all sorts of fish got caught, both edible and inedible.

It was necessary, therefore, to sort out the fish when the boat returned to the land.

Jesus came from a fishing community, and he therefore described something which would have been very familiar to most of his hearers. The parable teaches the same lesson as the parable of the wheat and tares (verses 49–50; compare verses 40–43). Not only is the same truth taught twice, but each time Jesus gives an explanation in case his hearers have not understood.

In verses 51–52, Jesus uses a picture to show that there need be no obstacle to coming to him for those who were experts in the Jewish religion. The teachers of the law and the Pharisees were contrasting Jesus' teaching with their own understanding of the Old Testament. Jesus wants his hearers to understand that the true teacher has learned to see the harmony between the two. Matthew in his gospel repeatedly shows this harmony by showing how the Old Testament points to Jesus.

Rejected at home (verses 53–58)

A new section of Matthew's gospel begins here, describing the reaction of various people to Jesus.

Jesus returned to his old home town of Nazareth (verses 53–54). There, for the last time recorded in Matthew's gospel, he goes to the synagogue, or the meeting-place of the Jews. Immediately his presence arouses astonishment. Despite his words and actions, his hearers could not believe him. The excuse is given in verses 55–56: their familiarity with Jesus and his family meant that they thought they knew all about him, yet Jesus upset them (verse 57). The result was that Jesus refused to do many miracles in Nazareth, just as he had refused to teach those who would not believe him and had spoken only in parables.

Matthew no doubt deliberately placed this incident at this particular point in his gospel. In the stories he has retold, Matthew has been comparing Israel to fruitless ground, and weeds, and fish that men throw away. Even the people in his own country did not believe in him, nor recognize his wisdom and his mighty works as evidence of the work of the Spirit of God. They did not know he was the Son of God, and that his true brothers were his disciples, not his physical family. So, sadly, they stumbled in unbelief.

Questions

1. Is it possible to think you know Jesus so well that you really fail to understand him? How?
2. Jesus clearly believed that a knowledge of the Old Testament was vital. Why was this? How can our churches restore it to its proper place?
3. Are there any 'popular' images of Jesus in your culture? In what ways do they 'domesticate' him, removing his cutting edge? Does the church do the same?

Matthew 14:1–12

Convicted but not converted

The sad story of a man who knew the truth of God's word but was too weak to receive it.

'Herod' was Herod Antipas, a son of Herod the Great by his fourth wife Malthace. He was ruler of Galilee, had married a daughter of Aretas IV of Nabatea, but then seduced Herodias, the wife of his half-brother Philip. John repeatedly condemned Herod and had been imprisoned as a result (3:3–4). Presumably he had pointed out that Herod had broken three of God's commands, having committed adultery (forbidden in Exodus 20:14), incest (compare Leviticus 20:21), and having divorced his first wife without an adequate reason (see Deuteronomy 24:1–4).

Understandably, Herodias hated John, so when the chance

came to get rid of him, she was ready to use her daughter to gain her ends. Salome (a daughter from her first marriage) was little better than her mother. For a princess to dance in the ancient world was unheard of, especially as such dances were usually sexually suggestive. But, though still only a young teenager at the time of this incident, she had already fallen into such an immoral life as to agree willingly to her mother's wicked plan. Subsequently she, too, committed incest by marrying her great uncle!

In 11:1 – 13:52, a large amount of Jesus' teaching was gathered together by Matthew. Running through all three chapters were two themes: faith and unbelief. A new section of the Gospel begins in 13:53 and extends through to 18:35. In these chapters a collection of Jesus' teaching and miracles are recounted. But before this, two separate incidents show an inadequate response to Jesus. In 13:53–58 the unbelief of the inhabitants of Nazareth was described. Now, in 14:1–12, we are given the response of Herod.

The Bible very rarely tries to prove that God exists, because it believes that, in the face of the facts, only the fool denies it (see Psalm 14:1). Thus, Herod knew John was God's messenger (see Mark 6:20) and that John spoke the truth. In fact, his conscience was so deeply troubled that, when Jesus appeared, Herod thought that John had come back to haunt him (verses 1–2). He had listened to John and protected him, yet he hated him, because other things were more important to him than peace with God.

There were at least three reasons for this: Herod was frightened of what his friends might think of him (verse 9), terrified of his wife, and frightened of the demands of God. His drunken lifestyle described in this chapter was typical.

Tragically, these very pleasures were soon taken from Herod. Herodias persuaded Herod to send a messenger to the emperor, asking for the title 'king' for himself. However, one of Herod's enemies also sent messengers who persuaded the emperor that Herod was planning a rebellion against him. Herod did not get his title; he was also banished to Gaul (modern France), and all his wealth and privileges were taken away. He lost everything, except Herodias, who showed there was some good even in her by staying with him.

Questions

1. What sort of people have you met who have responded like Herod to the truth of God? How can they be helped?
2. One of the most draining influences on many churches is the 'almost believers'. Can you think of ways in which this is true?
3. Are sexually explicit images ever acceptable in art, film or literature? Where would you 'draw the line'?

Matthew 14:13–36

The Messiah gives a banquet and walks on water

Two incidents in Jesus' ministry show that he is the promised Messiah and lord over nature.

In chapters 8 and 9 we saw that the miracles of Jesus were told by Matthew as acted parables. Here, in 14:13–33, two further miracles are described: the feeding of the five thousand, and Jesus' walking on the water. These miracles are also parables. In 13:53 – 14:12, two examples of unbelief were described (13:53–58; 14:1–12). The two miracles which now follow are intended to offer us a contrast; they describe true but weak faith and, at the same time, point again to Jesus' work and who he really was and is.

It is not surprising that Jesus sought a brief rest from his work (verse 13); he was, after all, human! In addition, after the death of his cousin John (see Luke 1), he was clearly reminded that his own end lay also in violent death, and he needed quiet to prepare for this.

This proved impossible because of his pity for the crowd which followed him. So he found time to meet their needs, rather than insist on his own (verse 14). However, the disciples, when they were inconvenienced by the crowd staying on late, acted in a harsh and unfeeling way (compare also 15:23; 19:13; Luke 9:49–50).

Jesus used this situation to teach the disciples their responsibility (verse 16). Not surprisingly the disciples complained that they could do nothing: they hadn't got what was needed (verse 17). Jesus, however, drew attention in the miracle to himself as their resource. The disciples' meagre resources were taken to him, and the disciples were then able to meet the needs of the people. The bread and fish, having been blessed and broken by Jesus, multiplied in the hands of the disciples. The Messiah was expected to be one who would provide a banquet for his followers. Here, in a totally unexpected place and way, Jesus did just that!

Living the truth (verses 22–36)

There are at least five lessons to be learned from Jesus' command of the storm.

- True faith always makes use of all that God has revealed. Faith does not merely confess the truth, but lives it out (verses 27–28). Jesus tells the disciples that he is 'I am' (a clear, if veiled, reference to the name of the God of Israel). Since this was true, Peter, perhaps somewhat recklessly (compare Luke 9:57–58; Matthew 16:24–25), makes use of what Jesus taught, to try and do something which was impossible.

- True faith sees every circumstance of life as a ground for spiritual growth and for the glory of God. This trial that the disciples had to face eventually led to their great confession in verse 33. They recognized clearly for the first time that Jesus truly was God. They worshipped him as they would only worship God. Moreover, Jesus reveals in this miracle that not only must the elements obey him (as described in 8:23–27) but here they are forced to serve him.

It is very easy to blame Satan for all our trials. Sometimes, however, our trials come from the loving Jesus who sends us trials to help us grow.

- True faith does not paralyse believers (verse 26) but, in trial, arouses them to action.
- True faith is sometimes very severely tested. It is easy to criticize Peter for looking at the wind and the waves. However, Peter's faith only began to fail when he was already doing what was impossible. But precisely because faith is faith, it will be subject to storms: fears and doubts will enter in. But, in such circumstances, the answer is to look back to Jesus.
- True faith is shown in complete dependence on Jesus. When Peter began to sink he cried, 'Lord, save me!' Marvellously, Jesus stretched out his hand to him and he helped Peter in his need. Jesus alone has the resources to help us. He alone is able to build up our faith. We must always look to him and come to him.

Questions

1. Where is Jesus asking you to trust him for the impossible today?
2. When should a church attempt something far beyond its strength (e.g. a building programme or a major mission)? How can we distinguish between faith and folly?
3. If 'the 5,000' represent the world and we represent the disciples, how does the banquet apply to modern life?

Matthew 15:1–20

Laying out the battle lines

Jesus contrasts Old Testament faith with that of the Jewish leaders, and the spirit with the letter of the law.

These verses begin a new sub-section within 13:53 – 18:35. The controversy between Jesus and the religious leaders of his day develops from here to the point where Jesus' death becomes inevitable.

The background to 15:1–20 lies in the Jewish leaders' understanding of religion. In the Old Testament, the great religious and moral principles had been revealed by God and had been illustrated by certain God-given rituals and practices. However, by Jesus' day true religion was seen merely as observing the rituals. This focus on rituals and practices had led people to forget why the practices had been commanded.

These rules multiplied and became more important than the Old Testament laws, which were 'broken' to uphold the new rules or 'traditions'. True religion had become concerned only with outward acts. It had been trivialized and, in a way, the leaders had made religion misleadingly easy: man himself could achieve what was needed. Yet, at the same time, they had made the religion burdensome with all its demands (compare 11:28–30).

Jesus cut through all this and went back to the Old Testament itself. Inevitably, what he taught would lead to conflict, because he and the religious leaders were teaching from two completely different standpoints.

Outer and inner cleanliness

With this background we can understand these verses. The religious experts came up to Jesus (apparently having made the journey all the way up from Jerusalem to challenge him, verse 1), and reminded him of one of their rules which Jesus' disciples were ignoring, ritual washing. According to the Jews, it was almost impossible to avoid ritual uncleanness. However, an elaborate system of washings had been developed to resolve this. There was a hand-washing on rising in the morning. Then there was another elaborate system of hand-washing, confined at first to the priests in the temple. Before they ate the part of the sacrifice which was theirs, they had to use these ritual washings. Eventually these washings were extended to all Jews who claimed to be truly religious.

Very often in a Jewish home water jars were kept ready to be used before a meal. The minimum amount of water to be used was a quarter of a log. This was enough to fill ten eggshells. The water was first poured on both hands, held with the fingers pointed upwards, and then had to run up the arm as far as the wrist. It had to drop off at the wrist, for the water was now itself unclean having touched the unclean hands. If it ran down the fingers again it would make the fingers and the hands unclean once more. This process was repeated with the hands held in the opposite direction with the fingers pointing down. Finally, each hand was cleansed by being rubbed with the fist of the other. A really strict Jew would do all this, not only before a meal but also between each of the courses.

Jesus did not directly answer the question raised by the leaders. Instead, he drew attention to the fundamental error of their religion. He pointed out that it overthrew God's word! God expected all people to honour and respect their parents (see Exodus 21:17 and Leviticus 20:9). The law was quite clear (verse 4). However, the leaders had devised a law themselves which enabled them to avoid this sometimes demanding responsibility, and in the cause of religion! Since God had a greater claim on them than parents, the Jews reasoned that something given to God by oath ('Corban', see Mark 7:11) could not be used for parents. However, the giver could use it himself as God's steward. In this way, a man could avoid a God-given responsibility on God's authority. This is the practice which lies behind Jesus' criticism in verses 4–6.

Jesus correctly diagnosed the situation (verses 7–9) by quoting Isaiah 29:13. These words had been spoken against the religious leaders in Isaiah's time, eight hundred years before, but the leaders of Jesus' day had not learned the lesson. In verses 10 and 11 Jesus makes a still more important point; a man or woman does not become spiritually defiled by ritual or ceremonial contact, since true defilement comes from the heart (verses 16–20).

The response of the Jewish leaders was as predictable as it was tragic (verse 12). Unable (or unwilling) to grasp the principles of true religion in the Old Testament, they had devised a religion which could only lead to hell ('the pit').

Questions

1. Can you think of any things that you insist that others should do to be 'real Christians' but which are not in the Bible?
2 Do you know Christians who teach more 'don't's than 'do's'? What do you think this passage has to say to them?
3. If 'almost believers' or nominal Christians insist on observing rituals which we regard as superstitious or unnecessary, should we discourage them or ridicule them, or should we see them as a possible route to real faith? Give examples.

Matthew 15:21–28

A world faith?

Jesus' remarkable healing of a Canaanite woman's daughter shows that the gospel means salvation for men and women throughout the world.

This is a very important story. In verses 1–20 we read of the Jews criticizing Jesus, and as a result Jesus had shown them that they were not really God's children but were going to hell. However, in this paragraph, we are introduced to a Canaanite woman whom Jesus welcomes. This would have scandalized the Jews because, for them, the most ritually impure person was one of the old Canaanite inhabitants of Palestine.

Although a miracle takes place at this point, Matthew clearly regards this as less important than Jesus' response to the woman. Desperately in need, she comes to Jesus, aware that he can help her as no-one else can. She even comes with some understanding of who he is (on the Son of David, see p. 138).

A deliberate contrast is surely intended here. The Jewish leaders had the Old Testament Scriptures, which were intended to lead them to see their need of the Messiah and to recognize him when he came. Instead, blind to their need and unable to recognize Jesus, they argued with him. This woman, without the advantages of the Jews, knew her need and knew Jesus alone could help her.

Verses 23–26 seem strange at first, because Jesus appears to be saying that the woman is asking too much and that he has come only to help the Jews. This view perhaps explains the disciples' harsh attitude in verse 23. They were still thinking, like the religious leaders, that the Jews had a special claim on God. However, we misunderstand Jesus if we think he believed this.

There are two ways to understand the passage. If the disciple's comment implies, 'Send her away without doing anything', then maybe Jesus voices the disciples' own thoughts and objections in verses 24 and 26. But, ironically, the faith of the woman (verse 28) shows her to be one of the 'true Israel of God' (verse 24), whatever her nationality. Then, because in the New Testament healing was often seen as a symbol of salvation, Jesus heals the woman's daughter. His words and his action tell her that God receives her.

The other interpretation assumes that 'send her away' means 'give her what she wants and get rid of her.' In reply Jesus pointed out that, at the present stage of his ministry, his work was directed toward the Jews. Yet probably with a twinkle in his eye, he encouraged the faith which the woman proved she had.

Questions

1. What groups of people do you sometimes suspect may be beyond Jesus' help? What hope is there for them?
2. Who are the 'Canaanite' women in your area and culture?
3. Do you think that Jesus would want us still to give priority to the Jews in mission and pastoral concern?

Matthew 15:29–39

Another remarkable meal

Jesus offers another banquet, but now to non-Jews. His kingdom is open to all.

This passage describes the feeding of the four thousand. Another feeding miracle may, at first, seem unnecessary (compare the feeding of the five thousand in 14:13–21). The two stories seem so similar that we need to ask why Matthew needed to 'repeat' them? A little detective work provides the answer!

In 14:34–35 we are told that Jesus went to Gennesaret, a non-Jewish area on the shores of the Sea of Galilee. In 15:21 Jesus is in the area to the far north of Galilee, near Tyre and Sidon. In 15:29–39 we hear of Jesus back in Galilee but, as verse 30 hints and Mark 7:31 confirms, Jesus is here still on the non-Jewish side of the lake in Decapolis. This is confirmed by a detail. The word for 'basket' used in 14:20 is a Jewish word, but in 15:37 a non-Jewish word is used (one of the incidental facts that shows Matthew is recording the facts accurately).

All this suggests that 15:1–39 describes the work of Jesus in largely non-Jewish country and that the feeding of the five thousand concluded his ministry among the Jews of Galilee, whereas the feeding of the four thousand finished a brief ministry of Jesus among the non-Jews or Gentiles.

Just as Jesus healed the Jewish sick who came to him (14:14), he does the same to the Gentiles (15:31). More remarkable, however, is the fact that here Matthew deliberately looks back to some Old Testament scriptures. Isaiah 52:7 foresees that the good news of salvation was to be preached on a mountainside; Jesus does just that (verse 29). In Isaiah 52:7–10 that preaching is described as leading to the salvation of people from all the world; in these verses Jesus is ministering to representatives of the non-Jewish nations of the world. In Isaiah 35:5–6 the final deliverance from the curse of sin is described in exactly the same words Matthew uses in verses 30–31. In Isaiah 25:6ff. the final banquet of God for all his people is described, and here on a mountainside Jesus provides a banquet. In Isaiah 29:18–19 and 23, God's people are described as having been made his friends and people once again. The Gentiles in verse 31 use the same language.

All this shows us how important Matthew believed these verses to be. Anticipating the completed kingdom of God, Jesus provides a feast for Gentiles, who are described as God's people. The identical banquet provided for both Jews and Gentiles shows that, despite the fact that Jews might think Gentiles only good for crumbs, they too can be full members of God's kingdom when they recognize Jesus as God's deliverer.

What does this passage teach about Jesus? There are three important lessons.

- Jesus brought good news from God. Behind this passage lie a number of Old Testament passages. Matthew's readers would have understood that Jesus is the herald of worldwide salvation and peace through God's redeeming activity.
- Jesus himself is described as accomplishing this salvation; abolishing the curse of sin. In verses 30–31 we have seen several remarkable parallels with the prophet Isaiah. Jesus' healing ministry is described in almost identical words in Isaiah 35, where the final reversal of the curse for sin is described. The feeding of the four thousand itself echoes the references to the final banquet of God.
- Jesus reconciles men and women to God as a holy people. The response of verse 31 echoes, as we have seen, Isaiah 29, where the people are reconciled as a holy people to God. Jesus is a Saviour who helps his followers to be holy.

Questions

1. Imagine yourself to have been a Gentile present at this remarkable event. Remember that Jesus was a Jew, with all that it implies (so you would imagine him to be prejudiced against you). How does Jesus 'come across' to you now?
2. How far should churches attempt figuratively to 'feed' the thousands of non-Christians who live in our neighbourhoods? What will attract them? Can we meet their needs adequately?

Matthew 16:1–12

The signs of the times

Those who *will* not believe are not to be convinced, whatever evidence is placed before them.

These verses are very similar to 12:38–42. The fact that Jesus repeated some of his teaching and that Matthew records it shows us how important the subject is.

Wilful blindness (verses 1–4)

The 'sign from heaven' (verse 1) which the Pharisees and the Sadducees sought is explained in 12:38–42. Jesus refused to give such a sign, because the signs already existed for those who were willing to learn from them. In ancient Palestine (as in other parts of the world today) a red sky in the evening was a sign of a fine day to follow, and a red sky in the morning announced an imminent storm. The Jews had learned to interpret such signs. Jesus calls them to do the same with him. No-one ever spoke like he did (7:28–29). His miracles, too, had never been equalled or surpassed (see the disciples' comment in 8:27). Even the demons had spoken of him (8:29). His whole life and work were already evidence enough. If that was not convincing, nothing would do.

In Matthew's words: 'Jesus then left them and went away' (see also 15:21). Jesus' action was an acted parable. He withdrew from those who didn't want him.

More blind spots (verses 5–12)

Why the disciples misunderstood Jesus' words in verse 6 is not known. However, Jesus' response is clear, as is the main point in the paragraph: beware of the teaching of the Pharisees and Sadducees. Jesus taught that the way people think and the way they act is closely related. Each feed upon the other. So the way that the Pharisees and the Sadducees thought affected the way they responded to him (see verses 1–4). He described their teaching as leaven. Leaven was a spreading, corrupting, evil influence, so powerful as to get into everything.

What teaching does Jesus actually have in mind here? He doesn't tell us. However, from what we know about the Sadducees and Pharisees, we might suggest the following things. First, the Pharisees had an exaggerated view of themselves. They thought they were super-pure and lived lives of great righteousness. This had led to a self-confident belief that they had a special relationship with God. Because they thought this, they could not see their need of Jesus.

Secondly, the Pharisees had a low view of God's purpose for the world. God desired all people to love him and to enjoy him. They had failed to understand this. Rather than delight in sharing their God with the rest of the world, they had developed an inward-looking religion which spent all its time concerned with details of legal observance.

Thirdly, the Sadducees in particular had underestimated the importance of the world to come. This led them to an exaggerated view of the importance of their present life. This, too, made it very difficult for them to receive Jesus.

It is easy, even today, to adopt views like these. If we do, we too will be in danger of thinking that we can get along without the need for Jesus.

Questions

1. Do you wish God would give you signs of his will? Make a list of the signs he has already given, in the Bible, in history, in your own life.
2. How far should churches expect signs and wonders today? When do they help the word of God to be heard, and when do they hinder it?
3. What things blind non-Christians today to receiving Jesus? How can we help them?

Matthew 16:13–20

Who do you think I am?

Jesus discovers how clearly the disciples understand his person and work.

Jesus had begun a period of ministry in which he taught his closest disciples more about himself. He had begun with a warning (verses 5–12). The question of Jesus in verse 15 is the climax of the discussion and it is a very personal one. 'But what about you? Who do you say I am?'

Who then is Jesus? The disciples provide some answers that others had been giving (verse 14). They exclude the very negative response of the Pharisees (10:25), but they quote Herod (14:2) and others, each of whose opinion was that Jesus was a great, even a unique, person. However, despite this, these responses were not enough.

Peter offers the conclusion which the disciples had reached (verse 16). They may not have fully understood what was said, but the confession makes some very important claims. 'You are the Christ' recognized Jesus to be the chief prophet of God. In Deuteronomy 18:15 and 18, Moses had spoken of a great prophet who would one day come, and through Isaiah (55:4) God had again promised a great witness. Peter clearly believed that Jesus was that great prophet.

The Jews believed that the Messiah would be a great, everlasting high priest. They based their beliefs on Psalm 110:4. They also believed that the coming Messiah would be an eternal king; a view based on another psalm (2:6). The disciples apparently believed Jesus fulfilled both these roles. In addition to this, Peter describes Jesus as 'the Son of the Living God': that Jesus was the God and Creator who keeps and sustains all things. The disciples were learning!

2:4–8 all believers are described as stones. Jesus taught that Peter's confession was the basis for being a member of the true church.

The last words of verse 18 ('and the gates of Hades will not overcome it') are not easy to understand. In the Bible the word 'Hades' can mean 'hell'. However, it can also mean 'grave' and, therefore, sometimes refers to death. In the ancient world a fortified town or village usually had a large open space behind the main entrance. This was known as the 'gate'. It was at the gate that people met together and took decisions about their lives and the life of their village or town. Jesus could mean that no plan made in the gate of hell would ever overthrow the church. However, if Hades means 'death', Jesus might have been suggesting that death itself would never conquer the church. This seems the most likely meaning.

For the Jews the 'keys' (verse 19) would have been clearly understood to refer to authoritative teaching. Thus, Jesus is saying, 'I will give to you, Peter, and all other stones like you, the message of God.' In response to that message, men and women would decide their eternal future.

Questions

1. Write a list of answers to the question 'Who do people say Jesus is?' What is your own answer? How do you justify it? How can you live by it?
2. What gods are 'worshipped' in today's society? Is your church totally free from false objects of worship (people, ideas, wrong views of God himself)?
3. What would you say to those who claim that it does not matter what a person believes, and that there are many ways to God?

Which lord is the true one?

All this took place near Caesarea Philippi, a town to the north of Galilee. Jesus had deliberately left Galilee and the crowds who had followed him to find a quiet place where he could spend time with his disciples. But why Caesarea? Caesarea was a very prominent religious centre, the focus of the old Syrian Baal cult; a cult which had made a god of all human pleasures, especially sex. But it was also regarded as the birthplace of Pan, the Greek god of nature. In worshipping Pan, men and women were worshipping the creation rather than the creator who had made all things.

Also, a great temple had been built in Caesarea for the worship of the emperor, where a mere man was worshipped as the master of the world. Perhaps Jesus deliberately chose this place where all these other claimants to lordship over men and women were powerfully present. It is in the midst of such a world that Jesus' call to 'follow him' is made.

Peter, the rock (verses 17–19)

Men and women, left to themselves, cannot see spiritual things clearly. When they do the credit is God's. Jesus reveals here a very important truth.

Jesus' words in verse 18 are a play on words. In the Aramaic language that Jesus spoke, *kepha* meant a rock but *Kephas* was a name. Many have suggested that the rock was Peter's faith. Others have thought that when Jesus speaks to Peter, he is referring to himself as the rock. Both of these suggestions are unlikely. How, then, was Peter a rock? The disciples, who were of course Jews, probably thought that Jesus was referring to a foundation stone. In Isaiah 51:1–2 Abraham had been described in this same way. Abraham was the first stone in the building of the Old Testament people of God. Peter, says Jesus, is the first stone of the New Testament church.

What, then, was it that made Peter a rock? The answer is surely the confession he had made in verse 16. He was the first person to understand fully who Jesus was and is, and the first of many who would eventually believe the same thing. In 1 Peter

Matthew 16:21–28

Messiah indeed, but a surprising one!

The disciples had discovered who Jesus was, but they had not understood that messiahship would bring suffering and death.

One can well imagine the scene. Jesus had now openly agreed to Peter's confession (verse 16), admitting to being the longed-for Messiah. The excitement among the disciples must have been enormous, and the desire to spread the good news almost unbearable. But Jesus forbade his disciples to speak of Peter's confession (verse 20). Why was this? Looking back some years later, Matthew finds two great reasons for Jesus' command. The disciples needed to learn the nature of true messiahship, and to understand what it meant to be a true disciple of Jesus. Only when this was grasped would it be appropriate to announce him

In Isaiah 52:13 – 53:12 the Messiah was described as a suffering servant rather than a great political leader. Thus, when Jesus speaks of his coming suffering, it is too much for Peter (verse 22). Peter had been brought up with the normal Jewish hopes so how, then, could Jesus suffer and die? So astonished was Peter that he rebuked Jesus. Thus the rock became almost immediately a stumbling-block; the mouthpiece of the Father became the messenger of Satan. Peter was unwilling to believe what Jesus taught, and this shows the wisdom of Jesus in commanding silence. If even Peter could not grasp the truth, then clearly far more teaching was required before the disciples told others that Jesus was the Messiah.

Jesus wanted to teach that his death was absolutely necessary. Later, Peter, more than any of the disciples, seems to have understood this. In Acts 2:23 and 3:18, as well as in 1 Peter 1:11, Peter describes the death of Jesus as necessary to fulfil the will of

God in Scripture. But above all, in Acts 4:11–12 and 1 Peter 2:21–24, Peter subsequently taught that the only way for men and women to be saved from their death was by Jesus' death in their place, bearing their sin.

True discipleship

Jesus calls his disciples to renounce themselves entirely, be completely obedient to him in everything, and engage in a life of total surrender and sacrifice (verse 24). Jesus was not setting a standard for some special believers but one for all those who would be his disciples and share his glory.

In verses 25–28 Jesus gives us three different encouragements.

- The life of true discipleship alone enables a person to live to the full. True discipleship is a life enjoying the favour of God.
- Those who follow him will reap an eternal reward (verse 27).
- The true disciple will experience glory even this side of death (verse 28).

The coming of Jesus in his kingdom is understood in the Bible to emerge stage by stage. In 17:1–8 the anticipation of Jesus' kingdom is placed before the disciples. Then, in Jesus' resurrection, ascension and in the gift of the Spirit, his kingdom comes. Finally, one day Jesus will return and complete his kingdom once and for all. Before they died, the disciples experienced the glorious fact of Jesus' resurrection life in them through his Spirit.

Questions

1. What have I lost in this life and what have I gained by being Christ's disciple? Does anything else have to go? Decide on a timetable.
2. Plan a service for your church on the theme of 'the coming of the Son of Man'. What will you include in it?

3. The world considers humility, suffering and weakness as failure. How far does that mean that the message of the suffering servant going to the cross cannot communicate to the world?

Matthew 17:1–13

Glory!

As he prepared for his death, Jesus showed three of his disciples a glimpse of his true glory.

After Peter's confession (16:16), Jesus commanded his disciples to keep silent (16:20, and compare 17:9) because he wanted more fully to explain to them the nature of true messiahship and true discipleship before they confessed him openly. This instruction began in 16:21–28, and here in 17:1–13 is continued in a remarkable and unique way. Doubtless the experience described here would have benefited Jesus, since it would have confirmed his task and strengthened him for the days that were to follow. But, as recounted by Matthew, it is above all seen as a means of teaching his disciples.

Peter had already argued with Jesus, despite the fact that he recognized Jesus as the prophet of God (16:22). Significantly, Peter is one of those chosen by Jesus to ascend the mountain.

There two very important things took place. First, Jesus had a conversation with Moses and Elijah. For the Jews, Moses and Elijah were the two great representatives of the Old Testament people of God. They saw the Old Testament as both law and prophets. Moses was viewed as the great law-giver, and Elijah was seen as the great prophet. In this context, therefore (and compare especially Luke 9:31), it is clear that Jesus was the one to whom both the law and the prophets pointed.

Secondly, the disciples heard a voice from heaven which echoed the language of Deuteronomy 18:15 and Peter's confession in 16:16. In this way, the heavenly voice emphasized that Jesus was (and is) the supreme mouthpiece of God to us. The lesson for Peter was: 'Don't argue. Listen to him.'

Matthew's account of the transfiguration seems to echo other verses of the Bible. First, it reflects the description of Moses' encounter with God in Exodus 34:29–35, where Moses' face shone because of his closeness to God. Jesus was transfigured by the close presence of his Father. Secondly, in Revelation 1:13–16, we have a description of Jesus in his ascended glory. There are a number of similarities between the description there and the event described in Matthew 17. This is, perhaps, not surprising, since John was present on both occasions. However, it suggests that the glory which the disciples saw on the mountain anticipated the glory of Jesus when his work was finally completed. In the days to follow, Jesus would be crucified before their very eyes. When that happened, they were to remember the events of Matthew 17. Peter had rebuked Jesus (16:22). Presumably Peter expected Jesus to establish an earthly kingdom. This experience was intended to reveal the true nature of Jesus' kingdom.

The glory which the disciples saw raised their thoughts and their ambitions far above earthly glory (17:4). If they had looked before for an earthly kingdom, now they looked for the full enjoyment of the presence of God.

The desire of Peter to stay on the Mount of Transfiguration is very understandable, but Matthew concentrates on the discussion between Jesus and his three disciples on their return. Once again Jesus asks his disciples not to tell anyone about their experience. The time is not yet right (verse 9). Only when Jesus was raised from the dead would the disciples be able to understand fully what had happened.

The section ends with a description of the disciples' question about Elijah and Jesus' response. Jesus had pointed out that John the Baptist was the 'Elijah' whom the prophets had predicted would return as herald to the Messiah (11:14). Seeing Elijah must have puzzled the disciples, especially as Jesus had been speaking to them about his suffering and death. This prompted their perplexed question. However, Jesus repeats his teaching that John was 'Elijah' and then makes the important point: just as John had suffered (14:1–12), so he, Jesus, must do so as well.

There is one final lesson. Jesus had said: 'I tell you the truth, some who are standing here will not taste death before they see the Son of Man coming in his kingdom' (16:28). This passage helps to explain these words, since the transfiguration anticipated the glory of Jesus. That glory has already begun to be shown for Jesus has been raised, he has ascended into heaven, and he has poured out his Holy Spirit upon his people. So, the kingdom of Jesus continues its advance worldwide; the gates of hell have not prevailed, the kingdom grows in the hearts of men and women in Christian fellowship and they, marvelling at the taste, await the full glory of Jesus.

Questions

1. How can this description of Jesus being glorified help me to be a more faithful disciple today? What points of contact are there between the three disciples and me?
2. The kingdom of God has already begun to come in power. What examples of this truth can you think of to illustrate this from the life of the church (even your church)? How is God's power exercised?
3. Imagine what would happen if Jesus showed himself 'transfigured' to every inhabitant of the world. How would the media react? governments? the military? industry? After, say, five years, would the world be a different place?

Matthew 17:14–27

Down to earth!

Away from the mountain we see everyday life – an epileptic not healed, and an argument about tax-paying.

Peter had made his great confession. Jesus' response (16:20) was to tell his disciples to keep this fact to themselves. The reason was that they still had much to learn about messiahship and discipleship. These verses develop the theme.

An inglorious failure (verses 14–21)

There is an intended contrast between verses 1–13 and 14–21. Three disciples had seen Jesus in his glory. The other nine had been left alone without Jesus' presence in the valley. There they had been called upon to exercise a ministry which Jesus had uniquely given to them (10:8; Mark 6:13, 30; Luke 9:6–10). Sadly, they failed (17:16), but Jesus was still the same Jesus. The failure of the disciples was not the weakness of Jesus, nor was it the result of his unwillingness to act. The boy's father recognized this (verse 15).

Why then did the disciples fail? The answer is provided for us in verses 19–21. In these verses, there is some difficulty in knowing what Matthew originally wrote. Some versions of the Bible do not have verse 21. It does seem unlikely that Matthew wrote these words. However, they are found in Mark 9:29 (although the words 'and fasting' are probably not words original to Jesus or Matthew, as most versions recognize).

Another difficulty in these verses is that it is not clear whether Jesus described the fault of the disciples in verse 20 as 'unbelief' or 'little faith'. Probably Jesus said the former. Most likely their problem was that since they had already undertaken such exorcisms, they had come to consider that they had almost magical powers. In this way, they had failed to exercise the living faith in Jesus which alone enabled them to do miracles and healing. Even a little faith would have been enough if it was exercised in the proper way, but here the disciples had sought to act independently of Jesus. It is not so much the greatness of our faith that is important as its genuineness, seen in humble trust and dependence on Jesus.

This is Jesus' point as he tries to encourage his disciples (verse 20) by using a popular illustration. In ancient Palestine, if anyone wanted to describe something as impossible they spoke of it as a mountain – something which could not be moved. Jesus, however, tells his disciples that when he planned to do something, even if it was impossible, they were to trust him and he would do what he promised.

Sons of the Living God (verses 22–27)

Jesus repeats his earlier teaching that he must die (16:21–22). But the natural question in response to this is, 'Why?' The strange events of verses 24–27 are intended to hint at the answer.

Every Jew was expected to pay a tax for the upkeep of the temple and especially the sacrifices (see Exodus 30:11–16). The sacrifices were necessary because of the sins of the people. All sinners faced eternal death because of God's hatred of sin. However, God had taught the Jews that he would forgive their sin if they offered up another life (of an animal) in place of their own. In this way, God showed that he was both holy and forgiving.

Peter is asked by the tax-collectors if Jesus paid the tax (a natural question, since some rabbis and their disciples were exempt, and the officials may not have been sure about Jesus' taxable status). Presumably because Peter had seen Jesus do so in the past, he replied with a 'yes' (verse 25). Seeing this, Jesus then told Peter a parable based on the incident. In the ancient world it was the common practice for kings and their families not to pay tax. Indeed, the same is usually true today. Jesus indicated that he did not *need* to pay because he was the Son of God, and because he had no sin which needed the payment of a sacrifice. But that was not all. Jesus also taught Peter that Peter did not need to pay the temple tax either, for he, too, was a son of God!

Peter had been brought up as a Jew, and Jesus' words must have astonished him if he fully understood them. However, Jesus then performed a remarkable little miracle to explain to Peter what he meant. First, Jesus showed that he knew all things and had power over all things – facts true only of God. Then, by the miracle, he voluntarily paid for himself and Peter.

This emphasized that Jesus did not need to face the death penalty for sin. However, in dying, he paid the debts of others. But there is another important truth here. If Peter no longer needed to pay the tax as one for whom Jesus would die, and if he was now a 'son', it surely meant that the temple was obsolete and unnecessary. Jesus' death would pay the full price for sin. Nothing else would be required. So, this strange little passage contains clear implications concerning the reason why Jesus would die. Once for all, Jesus would die for the sins of all his disciples, and he would make them the children of God by his death.

Questions

1. If someone says 'I wish I had your faith', how do you answer? Can faith be measured in any way? If so, how?
2. Where in the life of the church can you see evidence that people love to cling on to the obsolete, rather than live in the newness which Jesus brings?
3. Why should the citizens of heaven (see Philippians 3:20) pay taxes to earthly government?

Matthew 18:1–14

Who is the greatest?

Greatness among Jesus' followers will be measured by their willingness to be of no importance.

The disciples had much to learn and still thought in terms of status and power. This prompted their question (verse 1). The response of Jesus was to take a little child and use that child to teach two lessons.

- Little children do not relate to other children and adults in the same way that adults do. A young child will often mix with others of different background, class and colour, but they are often very good judges of a person's real character. This can sometimes be a great embarrassment to parents who have learned to judge others by standards which children ignore. For example, adults are often concerned about knowing and mixing with the 'right' people.

  In the ancient world children were despised. However, they often seemed to be around Jesus, and he expected his disciples to follow his example; the most despised, the poorest, the strangest, were to be as welcome to true disciples as anyone else (verse 5). True disciples must act in this way – otherwise they can never enter God's kingdom.

- Jesus taught a further lesson (verses 6–9). The 'little ones' may be his disciples, who show the childlike attitude of which he has just spoken, so, in this case, Jesus is warning against offences between fellow Christians. These are a serious matter! Or the 'little ones' may be children, like the child standing among them. In this case, Jesus is issuing a severe warning against all kinds of child-abuse – a remarkable statement, because the general abuse of children was widely tolerated in the ancient world. But 'the fire of hell' awaits all abusers of 'little ones' (verses 8–9).

Woe!

To the Jew, death by drowning was considered one of the worst ways to die, especially if the tragedy occurred far from their homeland. A millstone was a huge stone with a hole in the middle, which required an ox to move it. So we can see how vivid are Jesus' words which threaten judgment (verse 6). He describes a horrifying and completely inescapable death, and stresses that this is what happens to those who are not 'childlike'.

It would have been possible for someone to reply to Jesus, 'But aren't stumbling-blocks inevitable?' In verse 7 Jesus replies with an implied 'Yes' but adds, 'but that is no reason why you should be one!'

It was usual for the prophets to introduce a prediction, especially concerning God's final judgment for sin, by the word 'Woe'. Jesus does that here. People who claim to be disciples but are not childlike are heading for God's judgment, not his glory. An active concern for peace must characterize every true disciple. Otherwise such people are not disciples – except of the devil.

In verses 10–14 Jesus tells a parable which is the climax to his teaching here, pointing out that true disciples will reflect the character of God. Again Jesus may have either adults or children in mind here, or both. As 'little ones', all are objects of God's tender concern and care (see especially 14). This is emphasized in two ways.

- Jesus is saying, 'It is no small matter to despise those who have angels as their friends!' (verse 10). The Jews of Jesus' time believed that nations had angels but they had never suggested that children either as a group or as individuals had.
- In the parable which follows (verses 12–14), Jesus says that God rejoices like a shepherd over all his sheep, especially

over one who has been lost; how, then, can any believer despise other believers if God loves them? Rather, all true disciples must show the same attitude as the father or else they cannot be his children.

Questions

1. Can you think of ways in which you seek status among your Christian friends? How can you avoid these ambitions?
2. What kind of 'stumbling blocks' are we in danger of placing before others?
3. Does the non-Christian visitor to your church notice anything different about Christians by the way you organize your building and your services? What overall impressions do you think they receive?

Matthew 18:15–35

Caring and forgiveness

Jesus expects his followers to be concerned for one another, doing all they can to promote one another's good, and showing a forgiving spirit.

Dealing with those who offend us (verses 15–20)

Throughout these verses, Jesus describes a community in which all (not just the leaders) are responsible for one another! God's children are to correct an erring disciple (verse 15), but not from a sense of personal satisfaction at being able to point out the fault of another, or in response to a sense of personal grievance. The motive must be the desire to help the other.

It is not clear whether a sin against an individual was in Jesus' mind. The words 'against you' are not in every version. Whichever is correct, however, Jesus' words teach disciples to avoid both brooding and the silent enjoyment of another's faults. Brooding so often leads to bitterness and hatred. 'Don't brood,' says Jesus, 'tell your fellow disciple. Try to get the matter put right.'

Gossip arises when the faults of others are shared, but not with the person who has failed. It flourishes because faults are mentioned, not to bring healing and correction but enjoyment to those discussing the weaknesses of others. Jesus teaches that the tongue is to be used to heal, not to hurt.

Jesus was very practical. He also knew that bringing in another person with a different way of saying things, often achieved results (and still does). This explains why he gave the advice recorded in verse 16.

Yet sin cannot be tolerated for ever (verse 17). Finally, sin must be dealt with and conduct which declares a person to be living the life of an unbeliever must be exposed as such. Even here, however, Jesus' motive is kind, since action is to be taken in the hope that it may awaken repentance.

Verses 18–20 seem to teach that, where true disciples conduct themselves in this way, Jesus guarantees his authority, wisdom and presence.

Forgive as you are forgiven (verses 21–35)

A denarius was the daily wage of a workman in ancient Palestine. There were 6,000 denarii to every talent. The tax income from a small province like Galilee was about 300–500 talents a year. It is clear then that Jesus describes in this parable an unimaginably huge debt. Indeed, he combines together the largest number and the largest measure of money known in the Greek world to emphasize this! In the ancient world, a man would have been lucky to escape with his life if his debts were a fraction as large as those in the story. Jesus, therefore, describes a reasonable punishment.

However, payment of the debt is not merely postponed, as the man had hoped (verse 26), it is cancelled. What amazing mercy!

In this way Jesus intends his disciples to learn how merciful God has been to them in forgiving all their sin.

However, that is not the end of Jesus' story. The very same servant who has been treated so generously shows no such generosity to another, though the debt owed is pennies by comparison. Even though the same words are used as when he pleaded for mercy before the king (verse 29, compare verse 26), it has no effect. No wonder then that the other servants were distressed and the master angry at his conduct.

All too often people who claim to be true disciples reward God's patience with impatience to others, God's forgiveness with bitter recrimination towards others, and God's grace with a gracelessness towards others. But such conduct is not just unfortunate or difficult to understand. Those who claim to be disciples but do not respond to God's mercy by showing mercy make it impossible for God to forgive them. They simply cannot receive what they cannot give. So only punishment is possible (see 6:12, 14–15).

Peter had understood Jesus' words in verses 15–20 but he was still thinking, as the rabbis did, of forgiveness as a matter of calculation, not an attitude of the heart. The rabbis thought forgiveness should take place three or four times. Peter, doubtless expecting Jesus' approval, suggested seven. But Jesus' response shows that grace knows no boundaries, because God's forgiveness of us knows no boundaries. Graciousness is to be the way of life of the true believer.

Questions

1. Is there someone who has hurt you and whom you have not forgiven? What should you do about it? What would you do if they refuse to be forgiven, appearing incapable of recognizing their offence?
2. What does forgiveness *mean*? Is it a form of words; a feeling or determination to let bygones be bygones; a form of prayer?
3. Take time as a group to express forgiveness – either to one another, if appropriate, or to all those who *seem* to be unforgivable: terrorists, murderers, rapists, child molesters . . .

Matthew 19:1–12

Marriage matters again

God has instituted marriage for life, so he hates divorce.

Having finished the period of special instruction of his disciples, Jesus left Galilee for the last time and began his final journey to Jerusalem (verses 1–2). Jesus was still popular with the people, who were enjoying his miracles, but the authorities were increasingly resolved to end his ministry. They tried to divide his support and undermine his influence by asking a question calculated to catch him out.

Divorce was something of a time bomb at the time. Herod Antipas had recently divorced his wife (see p. 155), and John had been imprisoned and beheaded because of his opposition to it. The rabbis themselves were divided over the issue, some more strict, others more liberal in their views as to who could be divorced. None, however, doubted the right of every man to divorce his wife (subject to the proper grounds being established).

This explains the question which Jesus was asked (verse 3); they were trying to get Jesus to take sides in the current debate. Jesus' response, however, was masterly. He denied *any* right to divorce, appealing to God's purpose at creation, which established that marriage was intended for life (verses 4–6).

His opponents, however, were not finished. If this was Jesus' view, then clearly it conflicted with the teaching of Moses, and Jesus was rejecting the authority of the one who had mediated the Old Testament to Israel (verse 7). If this argument could have been sustained, support for Jesus was likely to have ebbed entirely away (which is what the Pharisees hoped).

Jesus' response again went right to the heart of the matter. Moses may have permitted divorce, but this was a far cry from making it a right (verses 8–9). Moreover, the reason for the concession lay in the people's sin. This was scarcely justification for making divorce a right available to all.

Jesus' next point has generated considerable discussion, and almost every word or phrase is debated. Since these words do not occur in Mark or Luke (books written for non-Jews), it is likely that Jesus' point was in response to a specifically Jewish problem. Perhaps the best explanation is that Jesus was recognizing that a marriage contract could be annulled during the betrothal period, where a serious offence against the relationship had taken place or where an incestuous relationship had (inadvertently?) been entered into.

So, he concluded, where divorce takes place and (especially) remarriage follows, the relationship is effectively adulterous as far as God's original purpose is concerned. We can understand the disciples' response (verse 10), but it is more difficult for us to see the point of Jesus' comments in verses 11 and 12. Probably, however, he disallowed the disciples' comment, and was making the point that the ideal of marriage is a demanding one to which everyone is not called, but it is not to be evaded when God has called a person to it. Generally, celibacy was rare in Jewish society, but (verse 12) Jesus lists those occasions when it may be appropriate; either from physical necessity or the result of special God-given demands.

Questions

1. The Pharisees were good at playing one scripture off against another to avoid the deeper challenges of God's word. How might you be sometimes guilty of this?
2. What implications does this passage have for the church's attitude to marriage, divorce and remarriage today? Is remarriage after divorce always wrong? If Jesus is against divorce, why do churches tolerate it?
3. Jesus was ready to challenge false ideas in his society. Where might he address his comments today? (As his representatives we are liable to be involved here.)

Divorce and remarriage

It is impossible, in the context of this book, to summarize all the different views held in connection with both this passage and the overall teaching of the Bible on divorce and remarriage. However, the following discussion does its best to offer some guidelines.

The Bible seems to teach very clearly that God instituted marriage for life and that divorce is something he hates (Genesis 2:24; Malachi 2:16). However, it also seems to recognize that, because of the effects of sin, marriages do break down and divorce sometimes (legitimately) takes place (Deuteronomy 24:1). It recognizes that, where a remarriage takes place before the death of the former spouse, 'adultery' (at least in some sense) occurs (see Jesus' comments here).

The main areas of debate concern the following questions:

- *What are the 'grounds' for divorce?* At one level, there are none, as Jesus teaches in Matthew; no-one has a *right* to a divorce. Yet divorces are sanctioned in the Bible, but on what basis? The answer to this question is not clear. Some suggest the evidence points to the adultery of the other partner (some also including desertion, on the basis of 1 Corinthians 7), others think a wider group of sexual sins are in view, and some would argue that the Bible does not offer specific grounds but that grounds are to be established pastorally and individually, when a marriage has irrevocably broken down.

- *Can remarriage take place?* Few Christians deny the possibility of remarriage (though many may sometimes doubt its advisability!). Some believe that remarriage is only possible to a divorcée after the death of the former partner. Still others think divorce makes remarriage possible (even if, against the biblical ideal, such marriage is 'adultery').

- *What do the words mean?* Lying behind the differences of view are difficulties in understanding exactly what the Bible passages which deal with these subjects actually teach. Such difficulties cannot be tackled here; but the difficulties ought to make us wary of over-confident assertions as to what the Bible does teach and generous to those who disagree . . . and, of course, we ought always to be very sensitive to those for whom the issue is very and painfully personal.

Matthew 19:13–30

Salvation and how to find it

Jesus reminds his hearers once again that to enter his kingdom it is necessary to surrender self and possessions to him.

Friend of the children (verses 13–15)

In this delightful little passage, Jesus welcomed those who were despised and neglected in society. But, typically of him, he used the situation to offer some deep insights as to the nature of his kingdom. In 18:1–13 he had emphasized that values within his kingdom were very different from those in the unbelieving world; sometimes such values were turned on their head! Once more, he taught that it was only those who were willing to be despised by those around them and happy to take up a servant's role who could be members of his heavenly kingdom.

Challenger of the rich (verses 16–30)

As Jesus continued his final journey to Jerusalem, he used every opportunity that came his way to teach some of his most vital lessons. In the first part of his conversation with the rich young man (verses 16–22), Jesus emphasized that it was only by complete trust and obedience in him that a person can be saved and enter God's kingdom.

The young man who came to Jesus was rich, upright and moral. Elsewhere we are told that he was an attractive person (Mark 10:21) whose riches had brought him respectability in the local community (Luke 18:18). Despite all these privileges, however, he was unsatisfied because he felt that he lacked a right relationship with God (verse 16). Out of this sense of need he ran to Jesus (Mark 10:17).

Jesus' discussion with the young man teaches two things. The young man clearly believed that he could gain God's approval by his own efforts. Yet, despite all his efforts, he didn't feel at peace. Jesus tried to teach him that effort is never enough. Only complete trust and selfless devotion to him is adequate to please God (verse 21). The whole of Matthew's gospel is intended to emphasize this point; Jesus' death alone can deal with the problem of sin. Self-help is doomed to failure. The young man's response in this story is tragic. Sadly he turned away from Jesus (verse 22). He remained unhappy but he found Jesus' demands too great.

Various attempts have been made by interpreters over the centuries to suggest that what Jesus is teaching here (verses 23–26) is deliberate exaggeration. He wanted to describe something very difficult. But Jesus himself clearly intends to describe something which was *impossible* and the disciples understand this (verses 25–26). This becomes clearer still if we take into account the beliefs of the Jews at the time Jesus lived. Whereas today we tend to think that God has a bias to the poor, in the first century the opposite was believed. A person's wealth and success were seen as evidence of the blessing of God. For Jesus to emphasize that even a rich man couldn't save himself meant that it was impossible for anybody to be saved by their own efforts.

However, Jesus then says that what may be humanly impossible is within the ability of God to do and is irrespective of human wealth and status (verse 30). Salvation is not something we earn but something we receive as a gift from God.

The young man had found Jesus' teaching too demanding, requiring too much sacrifice. But Jesus did not wish to give the impression that to be saved was all sacrifice and hardship. On the contrary, salvation is unimaginably rewarding for it offers, in the present life, joys aplenty (verse 29) and, in the age to come, all the blessings and riches and status that could ever be desired or imagined (verse 28).

Questions

1. What level of possessions ought I to keep for myself and family (present and future) and what proportion give away, either at one go or regularly over the years? How does this passage help?
2. How might your church present the Christian gospel as both demanding and joyous as Jesus did? How can we awaken the consciences of the tough while not crippling the over-sensitive?
3. What things hinder your neighbours and friends from receiving the gospel today? How far are possessions taking God's place?

Matthew 20:1–19

God's sovereign grace

God never deals with men and women on the basis of status, wealth or even service, but on the basis of grace alone.

From 16:5 Jesus' teaching has been increasingly directed towards the disciples, and he has been teaching them more fully what his followers should be like, and emphasizing what sort of 'Messiah' he had come to be.

Two incidents lead up to this parable. In 19:13–15 the disciples sent away young children, assuming that Jesus would not have time for them. Then, in 19:16–29, Jesus taught that status, wealth and importance are not the basis upon which God deals with men and women. Following the present parable two other events are described which help to throw light on its significance. In 20:17–19 Jesus emphasizes that he will be a suffering and despised saviour. Then he teaches that membership of God's kingdom is not to be sought for the prominence it might be thought to bring (verses 20–28). All this is emphasized by the twice-repeated statement (19:30 and 20:16) that God's way of doing things is often the complete opposite of human approaches.

Jesus' original hearers would have had no difficulty in identifying with his story. The situation he described was not an unfamiliar one and many poor men would have found themselves in a similar situation and desperate for a day's work.

However, Jesus gave the story a sudden twist (verses 8–15) to illustrate his point. He obviously intended his hearers to see that God was the landowner and the vineyard his kingdom (this was a popular Old Testament picture). Once this is grasped the point of Jesus' parable is immediately seen; all members of God's kingdom are treated fairly, some with outrageous generosity, because God deals with men and women on the basis of grace.

Matthew now reminds us, with a sudden jolt, that the generous master who treats all his workers so bountifully, must himself suffer hideously on their behalf.

Jesus, the suffering saviour

Jesus has already predicted his death and resurrection twice (16:21; 17:22). Here we are given the third and most complete prediction of his coming suffering and glory.

The present passage emphasizes the severity of Jesus' sufferings; he will know the disloyalty of his closest friends, the grossest injustice, insult and utter humiliation. All this will issue in his own agonizing death.

When we bear in mind that it is the 'son of the living God' (16:16) who speaks of his sufferings in this way, we cannot but be amazed! Yet in the present passage the uniqueness of Jesus' sufferings are not stressed (compare 27:46). Rather, Jesus wants his disciples to understand that his sufferings are, at least in part, an example. Like him they must expect to know weakness of body, experience exhaustion and pain, suffer bereavement and even their own martyrdom for the sake of following him.

Being a disciple of Jesus is not easy. The agonies that are common to all mankind are not evaded by being a Christian, and other burdens are added as a result of faithful discipleship. Yet, and this is surely the point of verse 19, just as Jesus gained his reward through suffering, so it is by the same road that the disciples reaches his glorious reward.

Questions

1. Imagine yourself as one of the people in the parable. Whom do you identify with easily? Do you find your feelings aroused by the story? Why? Why not?
2. How far does your church view itself as a community called to share in Jesus' sufferings? What model do we have of ourselves?
3. An understandable response to the parable of the workers is

that the master was unjust to allow those who had worked all day only the same wage as the latecomers. Explain God's justice, in the light of this story, as if to an agnostic campaigner for workers' rights.

Matthew 20:20–34

The predictable surprise

Jesus' followers are called to spend their lives serving others, not commanding them.

When Jesus was asked the question, 'Who is the greatest in the kingdom of heaven?' (18:1–5), he did not give a direct answer. Instead, Matthew recorded a number of incidents in Jesus' life and examples of his teaching which set out the sort of people that 'kingdom citizens' should be. In the present passage, all the earlier threads are drawn together to give a clear answer to the earlier question.

In the previous chapters Jesus taught that a true disciple welcomes even the most despised of people (18:1–9), is concerned for the least disciple (18:10–14), and even for the disciple who errs (18:15–20). He also emphasized that a true disciple does not stand on his or her rights but echoes, by conduct, the mercy received from God (18:21–35). A true disciple follows Jesus' words (19:1–30), delights in mercy shown to others without any thought for personal self-worth (20:1–16), following in all things the example of Jesus himself (20:17–19).

In the light of all this, Jesus' teaching is surprising. No-one else who has ever lived has taught what Jesus taught, yet, from all that he has already said, his teaching here should not have been unexpected. Simply, he says, 'greatness' in God's kingdom is not achieved according to earthly methods and standards (verses 24–25).

Humanly speaking, the request that James and John made through their mother (verses 20–22) was not unreasonable. They were members of the 'inner circle' of Jesus' disciples (17:1) and, possibly, they were cousins of Jesus (a comparison of 27:56 with Mark 15:40 and John 19:25 suggests that Salome was the mother of James and John and also a sister of Jesus' mother). In Jesus' world, it would have been considered legitimate and right to have exploited such contacts.

Jesus utterly rejects all this. Rather, he points to his own example of humble service as the mark of true greatness (see, especially, verses 27 and 28). For James this will involve martyrdom (hinted at in verse 23), and for John it will be exile far from his friends on Patmos. For all it will involve the daily routine of discipline, struggle, heartache and tears, especially on behalf of others.

The stooping, suffering Messiah

Up to this point in his ministry, Jesus has encouraged secrecy as to his true identity (16:20). However, as he goes to Jerusalem for the last time (20:18), the time for secrecy is at an end. The time had come for all that he had predicted. Thus he was ready to receive the acclamation of the blind men when they called him 'the Son of David'. The Jews used this title as a description of the coming Messiah. Jesus accepted the title without rebuke. Jewish hopes for their Messiah also included the belief that, when he came, the promised one would perform miracles. They based their hopes on Isaiah 29:18 and 35:5. Here Jesus performs a miracle which fulfils the Old Testament's predictions.

By both his acceptance of a messianic title and his performing of a miracle, Jesus indicates that he is indeed the Messiah. However, he was quick to show (through what Matthew seems to have regarded as an acted parable) what sort of Messiah he had come to be. The title 'son of David' had nationalistic overtones in Jesus' day, and the Jews had come to think of the Messiah as one who would bring national freedom from Roman oppression. However, by performing a miracle which fulfilled the prophecies of Isaiah 35, Jesus drew attention to a greater and more neglected part of the coming Messiah's work.

Matthew emphasizes Jesus' compassion (verse 34). This seems to echo Isaiah's visions concerning the 'suffering servant' (especially Isaiah 42:1–4 and 52:13 – 53:12). In those visions Isaiah had described one who was to come who would abolish the curse for sin by his own self-offering. Jesus was emphasizing that the true Messiah was not intended to restore the fortunes of the nation Israel, but would restore a fallen and sinful world by an act of sacrificial and compassionate love (see also 20:28).

In the imagery of the Bible, 'sight' is often used symbolically of spiritual vision. Matthew saw the fact that the blind men followed Jesus once their sight was restored as significant. The word 'follow' sometimes had a specific religious meaning describing a disciple. So those who have been given a true sight of the Messiah are to follow him by showing the same selfless and compassionate love for others as Jesus himself has shown to us.

Questions

1. How can you apply the teaching of Matthew 20:20–28 to specific situations in which you find yourself, at home, school, college, work or in unemployment, church . . . ?
2. How could your church better show itself to be a 'servant church'? Be specific again.
3. To what extent should concern for national and international social needs be a concern to the church and individual Christians?

Matthew 21:1–17

The Son of David claims his inheritance

Jesus' triumphal entry into Jerusalem and the temple reveals him to be the Son of God; a prophet, priest and king.

Jesus would have been well known to many of those in the crowd who were going up to Jerusalem to celebrate the Passover. However, not for the first time (compare 8:27), they begin to recognize there is something mysterious about Jesus. This leads them to ask afresh the question, 'Who is this?' The response recorded in verse 11 was inadequate but it was not incorrect. Possibly Deuteronomy 18:14ff. was in their minds as they answered; a passage that predicted the coming of a very special prophet, *the* prophet. Of that prophet it had been said that his hearers were to 'listen to him' for his words would be the very words of God.

But Jesus was more than a prophet. Throughout this passage are references that hint at something else; that Jesus was and is also a king. 'Son of David' was a title understood by the Jews to refer to the messianic king (20:29–34). Those same expectations foresaw the Messiah as a peaceful ruler like Solomon (see verse 5). Traditionally, palms were strewn before royal or near-royal persons, and clothes were cast before Jehu at his coronation (2 Kings 9:13). Zechariah 9:9 (quoted in verse 5), and its wider context, also predicted the accession of a king who would have worldwide rule. All these features, emphasized by Matthew, show that he understood Jesus to be the messianic king. Interestingly, too, the Mount of Olives (verse 1) was important to Jewish expectations of their Messiah. On the basis of Zechariah 14:4 and 9, they expected him to come from there and execute vengeance.

If the wider context of Zechariah's words are considered, it appears that the one who will come will be the Lord himself. This at once ties up with many Old Testament passages which speak of the coming Messiah as sometimes distinct from and on other occasions as identical with the Lord. In this way, the Old Testament anticipates the revelation of the doctrine of the Trinity and, as far as Matthew was concerned, reveals the ultimate mystery about Jesus; he is God made flesh!

True and false religion

The priests and the teachers of the law were the privileged religious class in ancient Israel. They were those who had responsibility for the temple; the place where God had said he would live. They had free access to the temple precincts and had the privilege of being instructed in God's word and were given the task of teaching it. The blind and the lame, however, had been excluded from the temple (on the basis of 2 Samuel 5:6ff. and Deuteronomy 16:16). Children, as we have already seen (19:13–15), had little status or role in the religion of the day.

So it is significant that Jesus teaches that the former group have desecrated the very place entrusted to them and, in so doing, showed themselves unsubmissive to the word of God (compare Isaiah 56:7 and Jeremiah 7:11, both quoted in verse 13). More than that, however, they are regarded as ignorant of the true meaning of the Scriptures they study so avidly. So when Jesus appeared, fulfilling Malachi 3:1ff., they were blind to him.

In contrast, those who had been excluded from full participation in the religion of ancient Israel, began to experience the very things that were predicted of the messianic age (see verse 14). God had accepted them and had reserved his full salvation for them. Thus they are described as coming to him while the chief priests and teachers were outraged by Jesus.

It is significant that Jesus 'left them' (verse 17). Just as the glory of God had left the temple in Jeremiah's day, so Jesus now departs from the temple, leaving those who stayed behind without the presence of God and under his judgment.

Questions

1. How easy is it for you to know the truth but fail to recognize what it actually means? Are there religious activities in your life from which Jesus seems to be absent? Give examples.
2. If Jesus is King, whose opinion is decisive in the policies and practices of your church? How does it work in fact?
3. What exactly did Jesus object to in the temple? Should we ever follow his example? Should the church keep quiet or overturn some 'tables'? Which ones?

Matthew 21:18–27

Jesus demonstrates his authority

False religion produces no fruit and is under the judgment of God. Jesus hints that his authority is God's.

The symbolic action of cursing the fig tree shows that false religion is under God's judgment. In April, the time of Passover week, fig trees in Palestine are usually without either leaves or fruit. However, on this occasion Jesus spotted an early flowering tree. For all its flowering, however, it bore no fruit. In the light of his experience on the previous day, he saw it as typical of the religion of the religious leaders; there was lots of show but no fruit. A living and fruitful religion alone pleases God. The disciples' question, when they saw the tree wither, encouraged Jesus to outline one of the marks of true religion: believing prayer.

We need to be very careful in interpreting Jesus' words (verses 21–22). Too often they are misunderstood and bring nothing but heartbreak. It is sometimes suggested that if only a believer has enough faith, then all that he or she asks for from God will be given them. Jesus' example is not intended to be understood literally, but to emphasize something humanly impossible. He is not suggesting that we can 'work up' faith to achieve anything we want. The Bible as a whole teaches that everything comes under God's sovereignty. Moreover, it is apparent that by 'doubt' Jesus here means fundamental unbelief in the revealed will of God.

Jesus, therefore, teaches that trusting faith, exercised in prayer, is able to achieve the impossible when exercised in accordance with the sovereign will of God. He does not teach inevitable blessing but encourages expectant faith.

Jesus turns the tables on his opponents

It is sometimes said that there are none so blind as those who will not see. This is vividly illustrated in the controversy with Jesus which is described in the passage.

By the time this discussion took place, the evidence to support faith in Jesus was overwhelming. We have already noticed that the events of the last few days had fulfilled much that was said of the Messiah of the Old Testament Scriptures. The healing of the blind men (20:29–34) had fulfilled Isaiah 35:5; the triumphal entry (21:1–11) the words of Zechariah 9:9; the prophetic act of cleansing the temple was in accordance with the tradition of Jeremiah 7:11.

These and similar acts had forced people to acknowledge the uniqueness of Jesus' words (Matthew 7:28–29) and actions (8:27). Gradually men and women began to grasp the truth (see 16:16). But then there were those who refused to face the facts (and they accused those who did of having closed minds!). Why?

The sad fact is the chief priests and the leading teachers come to Jesus with a question, but it is not a question to which they really want an answer. The question itself was not unreasonable (verse 23) but it is clear from what follows that it was a catch question. If Jesus had answered that his authority came from God, this would enable the leaders to make a charge of blasphemy against him. If, on the other hand, Jesus refused to give an answer, it would discredit him in the eyes of his followers.

Jesus was wise enough not to fall into the trap. His answer (asking another question) turned the tables on his opponents, playing them at their own game. He also revealed (verses 25–26) that their apparent interest in the truth was a fake. The religious leaders are shown up to be people concerned only to preserve their own dignity and authority in the face of others. This self-interest made it impossible for them to face the facts and learn from them, even though the evidence was all around them.

The whole story is tragically amusing. To the bystander the conduct of the religious leaders must have seemed like the foolish antics of clowns! The story is even more tragic when it is remembered that these very leaders were meant to be able to discern true and false prophecy. Yet, by their own confession (verse 27) they reveal themselves as unable to undertake the very ministry to which they had been called. Moreover, since they were ignorant, there was no basis upon which they could judge Jesus' ministry.

Questions

1. What encouragement can you find in this passage when people tell you it is stupid to believe the Christian message?
2. What does it mean for individuals or fellowships to claim that they 'know God'?
3. Why does formal religion so often appeal to religious people? What are its advantages? What are its dangers?

Matthew 21:28 – 22:14

Privilege and responsibility

Those who claim to be religious but fail to live for Jesus will be excluded from God's kingdom.

This passage recounts another series of three parables, all directed against the religious leaders. The parables pick up quite naturally from Jesus' previous conversation (21:23–27) where the leaders are revealed by Jesus as blind guides, unable to recognize truth when it stares them in the face.

Yes and no (verses 28–32)

The first parable contrasts religious leaders with 'sinners'. These leaders had, of course, professed themselves to be devoted to God and willing to obey his word. However, when John the Baptist (see verse 25) had appeared, they had gone back on their profession. Despite their fine words and their elaborate rituals, they had refused to follow God's messenger.

On the other hand there were those who had rejected God's words in the past (as their lives had only too clearly shown) but gladly heard John's word and willingly followed Jesus. The response of 'sinners' to both John and James had not melted the hearts of the religious leaders. The tragic consequence was that it was 'sinners' who were entering the kingdom of God while leaving the religious leaders outside.

An impossible ambition (verses 33–45)

The second parable is probably drawn from a real-life situation which was well known in ancient Palestine. Landlords frequently lived at a great distance from the property they owned. Their affairs were often left in the hands of stewards who were responsible for collecting rents and so on. This situation was one that was highly unpopular and of immediate interest to almost all of Jesus' contemporaries. But there is a twist in Jesus' story. The tenants quite foolishly (for the inheritance would never be theirs, see verse 41) kill both the stewards and the owner's son in order to try to make the vineyard their own.

Jesus explained that the story was an allegory; a story in which the details are each intended to symbolize something or someone else. The landlord is God himself, the vineyard is the kingdom of God (a picture already found in the Old Testament, see Isaiah 5:1ff.), the tenants are the religious leaders of Jesus' day, the servants are the prophets, and the son is Jesus. The lesson is then clear; the Jews would lose their inheritance in the kingdom of God because they had rejected the prophets (not least John) and were planning to dispose of Jesus.

Jesus was teaching a number of important truths here. Certainly, the story emphasizes that to be a member of the people of God is a remarkable privilege. There can surely be no greater status than to be a citizen of God's kingdom. Yet, privilege brings responsibility with it. We can probably identify three such responsibilities here. There is the need to bear fruit (verse 34b), the fruit of a righteous life (verse 43). Then there is the need to build upon Jesus as disciples who follow his words (verse 42). Finally, there is the need to be ready to hear and act on God's word (verses 35f.). In all this we need to recognize the danger of deliberate rebellion (verse 42a).

Jesus taught the tragic consequences of failure. To fail is to dishonour him (verses 45f.); to be numbered among those who killed him (compare 39). This inevitably leads to judgment. Yet, however much the church might fail, God's purposes and plans are not undermined. But how absurd to turn one's back on such privileges.

Ungrateful guests (22:1–14)

This parable is really three stories in one. Verses 1–7 tell the story of the repeated rejection by the wedding guests of their invitation to a royal wedding; verses 8–10 retell the tale of the way in which all sorts of men were gathered to the feast; and verses 11–14 recount the incident of the guest found without a wedding garment.

- In verses 1–7, the king is God himself, and the banquet a feast at the end of time for the Messiah. The closeness of this parable to the previous one suggests that the servants are the prophets (although it may include John, Jesus and the disciples). Emphasis lies on God's patience, the repeated opportunities to enter God's kingdom, and the stubbornness of those invited. Their response comes from a preoccupation with other (legitimate) things but, more seriously, the complete rejection of the authority of the one who issued the invitation. Hence judgment is assured (verses 5–7).

  Such conduct is inexplicable. No-one in their right senses turns down the opportunity to attend a royal wedding! Moreover, in the ancient world a wedding (especially a royal wedding) was eagerly anticipated and was a very happy occasion; the more so since it was one of the few breaks from the drudgery of everyday life.

- Verses 8–10 show that, since some forfeit their right to the marriage feast, all sorts of men and women will find themselves (to their great surprise) present at the wedding instead.

- The details of verses 11–14 are not immediately clear. Perhaps one person who had been brought to the marriage feast was offered a wedding gown (as was customary in Jesus' time) but rejected it. If so, Jesus intended to teach that 'bad people' are welcome to the feast but that when they come they must conform to God's will for them. Failure makes them no better than those who had been invited but rejected the invitation. Verse 14 probably emphasizes this last point. An invitation must be accompanied by actions which establish a person's 'chosenness'.

The message of the parable is pointed. The Jews (especially their leaders) had inexplicably and repeatedly turned down God's wonderful invitation. Others would take their place, providing they both came and conformed to God's will for them.

Questions

1. List occasions when you have said 'Yes' to something good and then decided against it, and occasions when you have said 'No' but then changed your mind. If the latter is a longer list, give thanks!
2. In what way do you think our churches are in danger of falling into the trap of existing for their own sake, 'claiming the inheritance' as their own?
3. If God has entrusted the world to mankind as his stewards, how far should Christians set an example in preserving the planet for posterity?
4. Make a list of the reasons many people give for not accepting God's invitation to his 'banquet'. How can we make the invitation more attractive without losing the seriousness of the matter?

Matthew 22:15–46

Choose your priorities

Jesus gives four examples of how to put God first.

God or the state (verses 15–22)

Sadly Jesus' parables seemed only to make the religious leaders of his day more determined to get him out of the way (verse 15). Once more (compare 21:23–27) they try to trip him up with a catch question. The radicals among the Jews believed it was wrong to pay any taxes to the 'pagan' state authorities. For Jesus to side with them might have provoked the charge of treason. On the other hand, to agree that it was right to pay taxes to Caesar might undermine Jesus' popularity.

His answer is a masterpiece of tact and clear reasoning. The question cannot be answered by opting for one or the other. Both God and the political leaders have their own spheres of responsibility. Thus, says Jesus, honour is to be paid appropriately to each.

The Christian believer lives in a complex world. Sometimes this makes the application of Jesus' teaching difficult. However, the principles that Jesus taught are clear enough and were subsequently emphasized by the apostles. So Paul in Romans 13:1–2 teaches submission to governing authorities and, in the subsequent verses, stresses the need for believers to be good citizens (13:6–7). Elsewhere he encourages prayer for political leaders (1 Timothy 2:1–2).

However, Jesus' words indicate that there is a limit to the powers of the state (verse 21). It has no right to interfere in church matters. Where, therefore, the state tries to take to itself responsibility in an area which is rightfully God's, the believer has a responsibility to God, even if this will incur the punishment of the state.

Bible-twisting (verses 23–33)

Jesus was surrounded by religious disagreements. Like the Pharisees in the last section, the Sadducees now try to trap him into taking sides in their dispute with the Pharisees over the resurrection.

The Pharisees believed in a very physical resurrection of the dead on the 'last day'. But the Sadducees rejected this belief because they did not find it in the books of Moses (the first five books of the Bible). So, appealing to Deuteronomy 25:5–6 and, apparently, Genesis 38:8, they asked Jesus another catch question. It was not intended to lead them to the truth, only to make a fool of Jesus.

Jesus, however, points out to them that even the books of Moses teach the truth they denied. He refers to Exodus 3:6. The

Lord is the living God whose favours to men do not end at their death. God had promised blessings to the patriarchs, to Abraham, Isaac and Jacob. There must be life after death in order that the patriarchs could share in the promised blessings. Since for the Old Testament believer God dealt with man as a whole (body and 'soul'), the resurrection of the body is an inevitable consequence of God's promises (though Jesus also rejects the Pharisees' belief in revived corpses).

Thus, the problem with the Sadducees was that in reading the Bible they had failed to 'think God's thoughts' after him. They had forced their views on the Bible, not listened to what the Scriptures themselves actually said. Part of their problem was their failure to have a proper understanding of God (29b–30).

If God is really what he claimed to be, then resurrecting men and women was scarcely a problem. They could only think about the future in terms of their present experience. But if God is God . . .

In a sense, we can understand and sympathize with the objections of the Sadducees, for they had never known anyone rise from the dead, not to die again. But those of us who live the other side of Easter Sunday cannot have the same excuse, or if we do, we can be far less confident of our views. The evidence for the resurrection of Jesus is very formidable indeed yet, sadly, people still will not believe the truth.

Love God and your neighbour (verses 34–40)

Jesus here answers one of the most important questions of all: how can I please God?

This particular question was one which the Pharisees often discussed. The Old Testament records 613 different laws (248 which encourage, 365 which discourage certain actions). With so many to choose from, which were the most important?

At first glance Jesus' answer is no different from the conclusion which most of the Pharisees had reached (compare Luke 10:25–27). However, he must be making a different point. The key to the difference lies in the words of verse 40. Very briefly, Jesus explains that all the Old Testament laws 'hang' on these two commands.

We can explain Jesus' point in this way. The Pharisees thought of the laws as many different bricks, each separate and largely unrelated, but with two bricks larger than the others. Credit was gained in God's sight by observing all the laws but especially the two great commands.

Jesus, however, had a different viewpoint. The two great commandments were like the mortar which made the other bricks into a wall. Without mortar the bricks were a useless pile of building materials. The two great commands set the standard by which all the other laws were to be fulfilled. Both the commands were two sides of one coin: love for God is seen (in practical terms) in love for one's neighbour, and vice-versa.

There is a world of difference between true religion and the religion of the Pharisees . . . and often between our own confession and how we actually live.

David's Lord and our Lord (verses 41–46)

The Jews believed that the promised Messiah would be David's Son. They believed that this is what Isaiah 11:1 and 10 and Jeremiah 23:5 predicted. However, their great difficulty was that they had failed to look at all the teaching about the coming Messiah in the Old Testament. In one of their most famous books, 'The Psalms of Solomon', they show that they had got no further than believing that the coming one would be a national hero.

Jesus here makes an attempt to get around this difficulty. He points out that Psalm 110:1 gives the coming Messiah a greater dignity that that of mere sonship to David. Rather, the Messiah is no less than David's Lord and God. The Jews had, of course, already showed themselves scandalized by Jesus' claims. Here he seeks to remove the obstacle by showing how their own Scriptures speak of the Messiah in terms he claimed for himself. And, of course, if he was David's Lord, then he was theirs also, and they ought to honour him.

Why did Jesus speak in this way here? The previous two chapters of Matthew's gospel have described the increasing hostility that Jesus faced. The earlier confrontation had emphasized the vital importance of love for God and one's neighbour (verses 34–40). In this paragraph, Jesus sets such an example of love by offering his opponents that knowledge of himself that would enable them to become his friends. In the following chapters, Jesus will speak only to the crowds and his disciples. Before the religious leaders leave and (as he well knows) go to make plans to get rid of him, he makes one final appeal in love. He does not use force or irony, but tenderly seeks to lead them to the light. Tragically, the religious leaders did not respond. They re-emerge in chapter 26 determined to put him out of the way.

Questions

1. How can I love God whom I have not seen? If I love my neighbour, does that count as love for God? Can the two be separated? How?
2. What value is there in having an established (state-backed) church? How far does Jesus' teaching in verses 15–22 help us to decide that question?
3. What familiar Bible texts do people use to justify their lack of commitment to Christ (e.g. 'love your neighbour', without referring also to loving God)? Make a list of favourite texts and ask carefully whether we are interpreting them correctly?

Matthew 23:1–39

Watch out, false teaching about!

Jesus warns his listeners against false religion which superficially appears correct but is not God-honouring.

In chapters 23–25, Matthew records some of Jesus' final teaching: first to the crowds (verse 23) and then the disciples (verses 24–25). These discourses are to be taken very seriously indeed, because people facing death weigh their words well. Though the religious leaders are the object of Jesus' condemnation in this chapter, he was addressing the crowds (verse 1), in a final appeal.

The first century was an era of innumerable religious cults. Nevertheless, it was not false religion but the perversion of true religion that Jesus attacked, and this is the more dangerous.

Jesus made the point that the Jewish religious leaders were heirs of the religious traditions that went right back to Moses. In so far as they did follow Moses, their teaching was to be put into practice. Moreover, the religion of the teachers of the law and Pharisees had been adopted by those who were very sincere and zealous: no-one else could have lived with its pettifogging rules and regulations. The religion of the teachers and Pharisees was apparently highly spiritual, and concerned for the right thing. Its disciples were zealous for righteousness, and it was a religion of the Book: the Old Testament Scriptures were the 'be all and end all' of Pharisaic religion.

But in all this lay its snare. Starting at the right place, it had turned true religion upside down, and discernment was needed to distinguish the true from the false. The remainder of the chapter is devoted in one way or another to Jesus' critique.

He begins by suggesting that perverted religion is burdensome (verse 4). It resolves itself into a long list of do's and don'ts but it offers nothing to lighten the load (compare

11:28-30). While the teachers imposed heavy burdens on others they found ways of avoiding the burden themselves.

Perverted religion has a defective view of the godly life (verses 5–11). It seeks power, honour and prestige. By way of contrast, however, Jesus points to the characteristic attitude of a true believer. As the servant of a Heavenly Father and of the Christ (verses 9–10), humility should characterize all the individual does.

Disaster ahead! (verses 13–39)

Jesus here exposes the faulty attitudes of the teachers of the law and Pharisees to the Word of God. He taught that perverted religion evades the Word of God (verses 16–22). Oaths were intended to secure that trustworthiness of men and women's words but the teachers had so interpreted God's Word as to make it easy to tell lies! Judaism at the time of Jesus was preoccupied with the question of what was a valid or invalid oath. Jesus cuts through all the discussion, and reminds his hearers that God's legislation in the Old Testament was intended to secure truth, whereas the religious leaders were devising ways of making solemn utterances which were meaningless.

Jesus' next point was that the Pharisees had majored on the minors. They faithfully obeyed all the rules of the Old Testament but lost sight of the principles which alone made any sense of the rules (verses 23–24).

True religion is a religion of the heart (verses 25–28). Jesus offered two illustrations. First, he reflected upon the preoccupation that the religious leaders had with ritual cleanliness and doing the right thing. However, they were indifferent to the need for the moral renewal which lay at the heart of biblical religion. Jesus' point is clear: only if inward change has occurred is any genuine change in a life possible.

The second illustration (verses 27–28) makes a similar point. Especially prior to Passover, tombs (which were not in cemeteries and, therefore, sometimes in unexpected places) were whitewashed so that no-one would be defiled by accidentally touching one. As such they could look attractive, but inside were only defiling bones. The trouble was, Jesus said, that the religion of the false teachers might look attractive, but it didn't deal with the underlying and sinful attitudes of men and women.

In addition to this, perverted religion refuses to listen to the truth. This accusation, made by Jesus, would have staggered the teachers of the law, of all people (verses 29–36). Yet, paradoxically, it was true. The leaders of Jesus' day prided themselves that they would not have acted against God's prophets in the past in the way their forefathers had. However, when Jesus and his disciples spoke the Word of God in their day, these leaders responded in exactly the same way as their forefathers had (verses 33ff.).

Jesus has had some hard things to say but they were not said harshly. Rather, like all true pastors, his words were only uttered with tears in his eyes for those who would not respond. So, amid all the perversions of true religion which have been identified in this chapter, Jesus bids his listeners to come to him and his word, lest judgment break out (verses 27–39).

Questions

1. Do you (or do other people) place demands on yourself that are not required by Jesus? Why do you do this? Is it because of conscience or what others will say? How can you escape this false guilt?
2. How can the church ensure it mixes tenderness with uprightness in proclaiming the gospel? Should we ever preach as Jesus does here?
3. How can the church show to the world the biblical character of true religion, when the world's assumptions are that religion is boring, irrelevant and oppressive?

Matthew 24:1–14

Waiting for Jesus' return

Looking to the future, Jesus describes what will happen to his followers so that they will be prepared.

We can find a parallel to the events described here in the Old Testament. Following the Lord's rejection of his people (Ezekiel 11:23), the glory of the Lord left the temple and took up its residence (temporarily) on the Mount of Olives. This was followed by the defeat of the people of Judah by the king of Babylon, and by the destruction of the temple. After the Lord Jesus' denunciation of the Jewish religion of his own day (chapter 23), he, too, left the temple (24:1), ascended the Mount of Olives (verse 3) and predicted the destruction of Herod's temple. History was about to repeat itself: except that this time there would be no second chance.

Jewish thinking at the time of Jesus would have associated such a destruction as Jesus predicted as marking nothing less than the end of the world. This is reflected in the disciples' two questions (verse 3): when will Jerusalem be destroyed, and when will the end of the age occur? Jesus answers them both.

Verses 4–14 seem to describe events that will happen in the entire period between Jesus' ascension and his return. Jesus warns the disciples not to expect his return for the wrong reasons (verses 4–8). It is easy to be deceived (verse 5). Jesus lists those signs which are to keep his disciples on the alert (they are the 'beginning of birth-pains'). We can readily recognize that wars, famines and earthquakes have always been around. There is no evidence that they are more prevalent now: nor is there any suggestion that Jesus thought so. The mention of 'false Christs' (verses 5) is, perhaps, best understood in this context. It has been a consistent feature in church history that belief in the imminent return of Christ has laid people wide open to the claims of charlatans. Jesus' words are directed, not to the world at large, but to professing believers.

Jesus' followers will often be beset by trials during the whole period before his return (verses 9–13). This is a warning against viewing these very experiences as indicating his immediate return. Almost always there will be some who suffer severely. Expectation of instant deliverance can be a great encouragement for a while during such circumstances and it is an attractive temptation. But Jesus' point is that it is a temptation. Comfort is to be found in the hope of final victory: not imminent victory.

All this does not minimize the severity of the trials believers will often have to face. Persecution, betrayal and death (verses 9–10), assaults from the outside, will be accompanied by attacks by the 'enemy within' (verses 11–12). Optimistic 'prophets' will deceive God's people, and prolonged trial will weaken the faith of many. Steadfastness will, however, be the order of the day (verse 13).

Evangelization of the world is the one great sign of the end of the age (verse 14), but there is no suggestion that it will lead to the end immediately. What Jesus does offer to believers is, however, consolation and confidence. Despite world-shattering events and the suffering and difficulties of the church, his disciples' mission (28:18–20) will succeed. And it is at this practical point that Jesus leaves off his introduction. Go ahead and confidently evangelize the world, he says, and let the signs take care of themselves!

Questions

1. How far do you see the return of Jesus as a threat or a delight? Make a list of what you might lose and what you will gain on that great day. Why do some Christians find it hard to believe in Jesus' second coming?
2. What would be different about your church's worship and evangelism if you knew that Jesus would return in a month's time?
3. What does this passage give us to say to a suffering, war-torn world?

Understanding Jesus' words

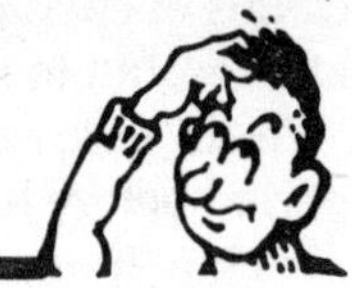

Matthew 24 has almost as many interpretations as it has interpreters! It is impossible to survey all the various views here. However, the following brief outline might help.

Jesus seems to be answering two questions: when will Jerusalem fall, and when will the end of the world take place. If this is so, verses 15–28 and 32–35 seem to refer fairly clearly to the destruction of Jerusalem, and verse 34 seems to date that destruction within the lifetime of at least some of those present. In contrast, verses 36–51 seem to answer the second question. This leaves verses 4–14 and 29–31. How do these verses relate to the larger passage? Since verses 29–31 are contained within a long section dealing with the fall of Jerusalem perhaps they refer to it, too. This does not seem likely, at first, for the language seems to be describing the end of the age. But is it? I think not (see below, pp. 217–218). Verses 4–14 could also have the same purpose: indicating the signs which would precede the destruction of the city. However, they appear more general, and seem to offer a timeless warning by Jesus against wrong-headed speculation concerning the timing of God's acts. The examples which Jesus cites (verses 6–7) were generally seen in the first century as signs of the end. Jesus corrects this viewpoint. Such events are far from the immediate forerunners of the end.

Thus, the chapter may be simply divided into three:

- Verses 4–14, a general warning against speculation about the timing of the end.
- Verses 15–35, Jesus' prediction of the fall of Jerusalem.
- Verses 36–51, instruction concerning Jesus' return: a call to watchfulness.

The simplicity of this scheme favours it. There is no reason to suppose that Jesus would present a confused and confusing answer to a 'simple' question.

Matthew 24:15–35

The fall of Jerusalem

Jesus offers some practical advice to those who would witness the fall of Jerusalem, and offers encouragement to those who follow to be faithful in evangelizing the world.

In Deuteronomy 18:17ff., Moses predicts that God will raise others as his mouthpiece. This prophecy came to be viewed as predicting one great spokesman of God, a messenger whose predictive prophecy would be fulfilled, vindicating his claims to speak in the name of the Lord. As far as the Jews were concerned, no prophecy could be more amazing and unbelievable than the prediction of the destruction of Jerusalem.

Jesus made very few predictions in his ministry. Those found in this chapter are almost the sum total (except his predictions about his death and resurrection). But he did make amazing claims about Jerusalem. Moreover, history would prove his words so correct that sceptics have concluded that Matthew must have written his gospel after the events had taken place! Jesus indicated that these events would occur within the lifetime of some of his hearers (verse 34). He was speaking in about AD 30. In AD 70 the destruction was complete. Most of the predictions in verses 15–26 can be documented with some assurance; not least Jesus' words in verses 21–22. No-one predicted the future like this man! Here was no mere prophet, but the incarnate Word (John 1:1–18). The destruction of Jerusalem vindicated Jesus: he was, and is, the great king over an international kingdom and a missionary people (verses 29–31).

Several scriptures are quoted in these verses: Isaiah 13:10 and 34:4 (as the NIV notes) in verse 29, Daniel 7:13–14 in verse 30a, and Zechariah 12:10–14 in 30b. In addition, the phraseology of verse 31 depends on Isaiah 27:13 (for the 'loud trumpet call'), and on Deuteronomy 30:4 and Zechariah 2:6 (especially in the Greek version of the Old Testament). These scriptures help us to understand Jesus' words.

Jesus' words are probably symbolic. In Isaiah, the destruction of Babylon and later Edom (among other nations) could be described in the terms of verse 29. How much more appropriate is such symbolism to the final destruction of Jerusalem! This may have been made more potent by the fact that Jerusalem is to be treated like the city which, in the Bible, symbolizes ultimate depravity and hostility to God.

The passage in Daniel does not apparently refer to the return of Jesus. It is symbolic language emphasizing the vindication of the one brought into the presence of the ancient of days.

The various allusions in verse 31 are to passages which describe the gathering of God's elect. Here his messengers (better than 'angels') do begin to gather together the elect of all nations through their missionary endeavours. Following the abolition of Israel's status (a fact to which the destruction of the temple bears testimony) the kingdom of Jesus is vividly described as a worldwide not a national community. The standard (trumpet call) is not raised to save the Jews but to deliver mankind from sin! Thus, as with 14, Jesus concludes with this confident prediction of the worldwide success of Christian 'missionaries'. The reliability of his predictions about Jerusalem should guarantee our confident service. They also assure us that we are full members of his kingdom and under his rule. The mourning of Jerusalem becomes our exultation!

Questions

1. What place do you think that the Jews have in God's purposes today, since they have come through so many disasters and survived?
2. How can your church gain encouragement from this passage? How secure are we from physical destruction (wars, civil wars, earthquakes, vandalism, etc.)?
3. Why has Jerusalem been a flashpoint in world history? What do you think will happen there next?

Josephus on the fall of Jerusalem

The Jews revolted against the Romans in AD 66 and General Titus besieged and then systematically destroyed the city in AD 70.

A brief dip into Josephus' *The Jewish War* bears out the accuracy of Jesus' predictions. The Jewish historian Josephus wrote of the siege and famine that occurred:

> Then did the famine widen its progress and devoured the people by whole houses and families; the upper rooms were full of women and children that were dying of famine; and the lanes of the city were full of the dead bodies of the aged; the children also and the young men wandered about the market places like shadows, all swelled with famine, and fell down dead wheresoever their misery seized them. As for burying them, those that were sick themselves were not able to do it; and those that were hearty and well were deterred from doing it by the great multitude of those dead bodies, and by the uncertainty there was how soon they should die themselves, for many died as they were burying others, and many went to their coffins before the fatal hour was come. Nor was there any lamentation made under these calamities, nor were there heard any mournful complaints; but the famine confounded all natural passions; for those who were just going to die looked upon those who were gone to their rest before them with dry eyes and open mouths. A deep silence, also, and a kind of deadly night had seized upon the city . . . And every one of them died with their eyes fixed upon the Temple.

Josephus also tells a story of a woman who killed and roasted her suckling child and says that 'when the Romans were come to the houses to plunder them, they found entire families of dead men, and the upper rooms full of dead corpses . . . [Such hardened men] stood on the horror of this sight, and went out without touching anything'.

97,000 were taken captive, but over 110,000 died.

Matthew 24:36 – 25:13

Coming again. Be prepared!

Jesus prepares his followers for his final return.

Verses 36–51 are a call to all Jesus' disciples to be prepared for the end which Jesus predicts here. Chapter 25 contains three parables which reinforce his message.

Jesus tells us that his second coming will be totally unexpected; unbelievers will be unprepared (verses 38–41). However, believers themselves will be taken by surprise (verse 44b) and, quite amazingly, even Jesus himself is not privy to the secret (verse 36).

The last point raises questions about the relationships which exist within the Godhead. Thus, Christians have invariably been mystified by this statement; even to the extent of emending the Greek text! But one thing is clear: all speculation about the timing of the end is both futile and blasphemous, enquiring into things forbidden by God himself.

The unexpectedness of Jesus' return demands constant watchfulness. Jesus warned against futile speculation about the end and offered no signs at all. So watchfulness must not be a matter of scrutinizing signs. What is vital is constant preparedness, not found in quiet waiting but in regular faithful stewardship (verses 45–47). Christians are to be diligent about all the duties they have as citizens, church members and, above all, as witnesses to a lost world. Nothing is ever to override these responsibilities. Indeed, defaulters will lose their hope of glory (verses 48–51). This does not mean that salvation is by works, but it does teach that true salvation is witnessed by persevering and undistracted service.

Once again, therefore, we find Jesus calling his disciples away from anything which might distract them from their duty. Verses 14, 35 and 45ff. have all concluded at the same point. Jesus is coming. That is the one certain thing. Be content with that knowledge, says Jesus, and get on with reaching the lost and doing all your duties. 'Go labour on,' says Jesus, 'I am coming: depend on that. In the meanwhile, persevere and take this blessed assurance with you to strengthen you wherever I lead you.'

The wise and the foolish

In a Palestinian village (then and now) a wedding was a great occasion where the whole community would turn out to accompany the married couple to their new home. Often the longest route was taken so that the couple might receive the good wishes of the maximum number of people!

A newly married couple would not go away for a honeymoon but would stay at home where they kept open house for a week and where they were treated (and even addressed) like royalty. Only chosen friends, however, were admitted to the celebrations. Frequently a bridegroom would delay his arrival to see if he could catch the guests 'napping', and in order to do this he might sometimes arrive during the night. Whenever he arrived, the guests were expected to go out and meet him and join in the celebrations, bearing torches if he came at night.

This forms the background to Jesus' parable. Jesus would seem to have had the following lessons in mind as he told his story.

- There would be many who would await his own return and who would appear indistinguishable from one another. The story describes ten girls all excitedly waiting for the return of the bridegroom.
- A large proportion of those people would gain the

blessings which they so eagerly looked forward to. The five girls who had not brought adequate oil reserves were foolish and unprepared. Jesus clearly wanted to emphasize the vital importance of sustained, diligent preparation among his disciples while they waited for his return.

- True religion cannot be 'borrowed'. The foolish girls could not get into the banquet because others were prepared when they were not.
- Finally, there will come a time when it is too late to change. That time may well take people by surprise (as it did the foolish girls) by its suddenness.

Jesus' parable offered a very simple illustration. Today it is intended to challenge those who claim to be Christians. Are you and I ready for our 'bridegroom's' return?

Questions

1. In what ways are you making ready for Jesus?
2. What are the main issues of debate or disagreement in your church? How important are they in view of the coming end of the world?
3. If Jesus' return is delayed that long, what will life be like in 2050? Should we be preparing for that?

Matthew 25:14–30

Called to faithful service

While disciples await Jesus' return, they should be actively at work, so that when he comes he will be pleased with them.

Verses 1–13 are intended to ensure that Jesus' followers 'keep watch'. In the second parable in this chapter, Jesus shows how this is to be done.

This story in verses 14–30 is about slaves (not 'servants', as in the NIV), people with no rights of their own but only duties and responsibilities to their master. Jesus reminds his listeners that they are to view themselves as his slaves (not a popular idea today). Yet, the service of God is a responsible work. This is emphasized in a number of ways by Jesus' story. The master was wonderfully generous in his estimate of the abilities of his servants and in the responsibility he delegated to them. A talent was 6,000 dinars and was worth a vast sum of money: probably equivalent to twenty years' wages for the average worker. However, in the story, the least that any slave was entrusted with was one talent.

These talents were given by the master to be used on his behalf. When he returned from his journey it was so that he could settle accounts (verse 19). During the intervening time, he expected his slaves to have made a profit from the money which he had entrusted to them. Jesus' point is simple; God gives gifts to all his children so that they can serve him by using those gifts to the full. The talents, skills and opportunities which each follower of Jesus is given are in proportion to their ability to carry and use them.

A feature of Jesus' story is that the master appeared to be equally pleased with each of the slaves who had done their best. Each of the first two slaves were rewarded 100% and praised in the same way (verses 21, 23). The master was clearly more interested in the effort each had put in than in the results that each had achieved. There could be no excuse for being lazy if the master was so generous! No wonder the delight of the first two slaves could scarcely know any bounds.

However, there was another slave. In ancient Palestine a law stated that 'whoever immediately buries property entrusted to him is no longer liable because he has taken the safest course conceivable; the man who merely binds it up in a cloth is punished if it is lost'. This helps us to understand the third slave's motive; he was concerned to take the safest course to protect himself. Jesus' point was that this slave was merely concerned to 'keep the slate clean'. He had no affection for his master, nor had he any real interest in serving him.

But the safe way proved to be disastrous (verses 26–30). Jesus' language in these verses goes well beyond the original illustration to pick up the idea of the final judgment. His point could not be clearer; those professing followers who show no interest in serving him and using their gifts to the full, but who are merely interested in securing their own salvation from hell, will find themselves, at the time of the judgment, in the very place they have carefully sought to avoid.

Questions

1. How do you react to being described as a 'slave' for God? (Slaves were often allowed wide initiatives and heavy responsibilities.)
2. How does your church encourage its members to use to the full all the gifts that God has given them?
3. The world sees Christians as simply interested in 'saving our souls' or at best as 'do-gooders'. How do we react to these views?

Matthew 25:31–46

Serving at the kitchen sink

True service is humble service right where we are.

Jesus appealed to his followers to be watchful (24:42), to be prepared (verses 1–13) and to serve him (verses 14–30). This shows the sort of service which Jesus requires of his followers.

Drawing upon the language of Daniel 7, Jesus describes God's throne set up for his final judgment of everyone (verses 31–32). This judgment will divide mankind into two groups on the basis of what they have done in their lives.

No sins are mentioned in this story. The group who are condemned are not judged on the basis of sins they have committed but of duties neglected (verses 41–43). Christian theologians have sometimes distinguished between passive and active obedience. Passive obedience is the avoidance of acts of sin, but active obedience is the pursuit of all those things which God delights to see in one of his children. Jesus appears to be making precisely this point here; the uncalculated response of love to all those in need is expected of every true follower (verses 37–39).

In ancient Palestine sheep and goats were virtually indistinguishable. While Jesus' followers too may appear to be very like one another, the judgment will reveal those who have truly served him and those who have merely claimed to follow him. Close inspection reveals a huge difference between the true and false disciple.

When duties are mentioned there are always those who will bind back-breaking burdens upon the sensitive and unwary. Jesus was aware of this, recognizing that most of his followers were never likely to be able to solve some of the world's greatest problems. So his illustrations are drawn from the insignificant and humdrum (verses 35–36), situations in which we can find ourselves almost daily. Jesus' point is that it is in the humble discharge of our day-to-day lives that we are to serve him.

Jesus also stresses how such active obedience is very precious to him. Small accomplishments are accompanied by enormous rewards (verse 34), and the least service of others is seen as rendered to him (verse 40). More than this, however, he indicates that only this sort of conduct will secure his favour. Jesus did not intend to suggest that we are saved by what we do, but he does teach that our salvation will be clearly confirmed only where humble service is seen. Those who fail here are heirs not of heaven but of hell (46), however much they may protest (verses 44, 46).

Questions

1. What can I do today to serve Jesus? Do I need to change my plans in view of my answer? Why, or why not?
2. In this parable people are judged by what they have done (or failed to do). How does this square with the truth that we are saved not by works but by God's grace? Where does faith come in?
3. Are Jesus' 'brothers' (verses 40, 45) all who are in need, or simply Christians? Consider the practical implications of your answer.

Matthew 26:1–16

Nearing the end

As Jesus consciously draws near to the end of his life, various responses show the right and wrong ways to react to him.

With a deep breath Matthew now begins to describe the events which formed the climax of Jesus' ministry. The time for words is now effectively past: the final and great act of Jesus to secure the redemption of his people is now at hand (verse 2). With great skill Matthew tells his story. He recounts several incidents, not apparently in chronological order, to bring out some important and instructive contrasts: Jesus' own sovereign and voluntary act is set side by side with the plans of men (verses 1–5); the response of the religious leaders is contrasted with that of Mary of Bethany (verses 6-13); and she is then contrasted with Judas (verses 14–16).

The climax of Jesus' work was his voluntary offering for sin. Earlier in his ministry Jesus had predicted his death (16:21; 17:22–23; 20:18–20). But now he predicts both the time and the means of death (verse 2). In this way he emphasizes that he is in total control; his death would be no accident of history. It was his deliberate plan and purpose to die. But Jesus also reveals the nature of his death: he will be 'the Paschal Lamb by God appointed', the supreme sacrifice offered to save his people from the wrath of God.

Jesus' passion (suffering) is the supreme example of his teaching. His words in verse 1 probably apply to all of his teaching earlier in the gospel (certainly to the previous two chapters). Having shown in 25:31–46 how his disciples are to be watchful for his return by their selfless love, Jesus now demonstrates his 'careless' love for his people. In the remainder of this section two inadequate responses to Jesus (verses 3–5,

14–16) flank the commendable example of Mary (verses 6–13).

Caiaphas illustrates the response of those inconvenienced by the ministry of Jesus. Caiaphas is known from first-century historians as a man obsessed by the pursuit of power. Thus, he and his colleagues are anxious to eliminate the threat of the one who claimed authority over them.

In marked contrast Matthew records a lovely example of true love for Jesus (verses 6–13). We ought to be grateful for the example of Mary of Bethany (compare John 12:3), or else we might be tempted to view Jesus' own example as too much beyond our reach. Mary seems to have been one of the best hearers that Jesus ever had (see Luke 10:38–42). She seems to have acted in full knowledge of Jesus' imminent death, since spikenard (so John and Mark record the type of perfume) was used especially for anointing the dead. However, whatever Mary may or may not have understood, her extravagant act of love is the focus of the story. In John 12:5 we are told the perfume was worth 300 denarii, or nearly a year's wages.

The last response to Jesus mentioned by Matthew is that of the disillusioned (verses 14–16). We cannot really be sure why Judas acted as he did, but it seems that Judas was unhappy with Jesus because he failed to provide Judas with what he thought he should get out of discipleship. For that he was willing to turn traitor.

Questions

1. To what extent are you a 'Mary' kind of person? How far do we need to demonstrate our devotion publicly?
2. If we re-enacted Mary's devotion today, in church, what would be lacking? Spontaneity? Reality? Love? Was it unrepeatable? What similar things should we be doing that are real?
3. Traitors are described as Judases. What were Judas' motives for betraying Christ? How many of them do we share?

Matthew 26:17–30

'This is my blood'

In the last supper Jesus explains the meaning of his imminent death.

In the last study the sovereignty of Jesus was contrasted with the tragic response of men to him! This theme continues. Jesus reveals his knowledge that one of his disciples will betray him and that he knows who it will be (verse 25). Then the focus in these verses shifts to a fuller explanation of Jesus' death.

We cannot escape the threefold repetition in verses 17, 18 and 19 of the word 'Passover'. Matthew clearly intends us to understand that Jesus hosts a Passover meal (verses 26–30). Moreover, verse 2 has already indicated that Jesus intended to die at Passover. John's gospel indicates, in fact, that Jesus died on the day before Passover, at the very time that the Passover lambs were being killed. Thus, Jesus celebrated his own Passover a day earlier than the 'official' event (there do seem to have been slightly different calendars used for the celebration of Passover during the time of Jesus). All this emphasizes that Jesus intended his death to be seen as a fulfilment of the Passover. This being so, we can make the following observations:

- His death was 'vicarious', that is, he died for the benefit of others. That was true of the Passover lamb which was slain (originally) to secure the life of every firstborn Israelite from the Lord's avenging angel. The allusion in verse 28 to Isaiah 52:13 – 53:12 ('poured out' alludes to Isaiah 53:10) makes the same point.
- Verse 28 goes further. Jesus' death was an offering for sin. When Jesus died, he died for others because of their sin.

- As such he died as a substitute and a penal offering. This means that he bore the avenging wrath of God against sin in place of others. These last three aspects of his work on the cross are seduced by 'blood' (verse 28a). This was the significance of blood sacrifice in the Old Testament and the same imagery is used here.

How does Jesus' death apply to us?

But how could all this actually bring men and women forgiveness from God? The answer is that God can and does forgive sin because the full penalty for sin has been paid (there can be no greater penalty than death, verse 28). In addition, God *forgets* sin. Verse 28a alludes to Jeremiah 31:31–34 where God says 'I will remember their sins no more'.

But it is not simply that Jesus' death brings the hostility between himself and mankind to an end. Rather, he died to make us the family and friends of God. This is the point of verse 29. Jesus describes the messianic banquet. In the ancient world such a banquet was open only to friends or to members of the family. That Jesus is speaking of a family relationship here is emphasized by his use of the words the 'blood of the covenant'; words which look back to Exodus 24:8 where God made Israel 'his family'.

Also note that Jesus' offering was 'particular'; he died 'for many'. This means that he did not die in general for all (though there is something of that in his death on the cross, since *all* who come will find his blood is effective for them), but actually for individuals. Thus when a Christian says 'Jesus died for me', he or she means just that. He died for an innumerable host of specific individuals. What a marvellous thing Jesus did when he died! What more could he have done than to meet these, our greatest, needs. Acceptance, peace, forgiveness, love are all ours and at the hand of God himself . . . Yet the benefits of Jesus' death must be received (verse 26). We do not automatically become the beneficiaries of his death. We must 'eat and drink': a symbolic phrase which emphasizes our complete identification with his death through our total trust in his death as the only way to God.

One final observation on this passage regarding the 'exceeding sinfulness of sin'. There is some doubt as to whether Judas remained for the 'Lord's Table'. What is clear is that he had the truth of Jesus' death clearly set before him, that he experienced the tender loving appeal of Jesus (surely the main purpose of verses 20–25) and yet, knowingly, betrayed Jesus!

Questions

1. How do you answer the critic who says 'If God is a God of love, he will not allow anyone to remain out of heaven for ever'?
2. When you meet with others around the Lord's Table, what are the truths that you ought to have in mind? How far is the effectiveness of Communion dependant on your thoughts at the time? Discuss your ideas in the light of Jesus' teaching here.
3. If Jesus died for the world (see John 3:16), why is the world not saved?

Matthew 26:31–56

'Your will be done!'

In these solemn verses, the sheer necessity and cost of Jesus' death is vividly described.

As we follow in the footsteps of Jesus and his disciples to the Garden of Gethsemane, we cannot escape the feeling that here we are on holy ground. Something awesome and beyond words is described here. If verses 1–16 emphasized the fact of the coming death of Jesus and verses 17–29 explained the reason for his death, these verses set before us the sheer necessity and cost of that death.

The agony

Nowhere else in the passion story are we brought so closely face to face with the agonies through which Jesus went because of the cross. We are told that Jesus was 'sorrowful and troubled' but this hardly does justice to the expression of utter wretchedness which is implied here. This is brought out in the New International Version by the words, 'My soul is overwhelmed with sorrow' (verse 38), and Jesus' words 'to the point of death' bring out the utter turmoil in his mind and heart. It was surely for this reason that he sought the company of his dearest friends; he just wanted them to be there and to watch and pray with him.

Jesus thus experienced the depth of agony and despair which is the common lot of men and women in extremity, especially when faced with death. And yet it was more than that! Perhaps we are inclined to think that, because he was God as well as man, he did not, or could not, feel the agony that is sometimes ours. In fact, as this passage shows, the reverse is true, since for Jesus the agony was made greater by his foreknowledge (verse

39). It is a mark of God's grace towards us that we do not know the future. If we did, the agony of impending disaster would sometimes be more than we could bear. But Jesus knew all that lay ahead and his agony was made greater because he was to be handed over to sinners (verse 45). He was the holy God who could not bear to look at sin. Now, he was to be manhandled to the point of death by the people he had created!

In addition to all of this, he knew beforehand that he would be betrayed (verses 21–25 and 46–50) and abandoned even by his dearest friends (verses 31ff., 56). Finally, there was the added agony of knowing that, though a pathway of escape existed (verse 53; a legion was 6,000 men), he must follow the path that would lead to his death.

The necessity

This passage also emphasizes the necessity of the way of the cross. Jesus did discover peace in the midst of his trial and strength to go forward, yet death was no more something he looked forward to than it is for us. He longed to gain the crown without the pain (verse 39). Yet, the Father's 'helplessness' shows us that there was no other way to bring men and women to God. The New Testament writers understood this well (see Acts 4:12). Nothing in the Bible emphasizes, as these verses do, the absolute necessity of our finding peace with God through Jesus.

This fact is further emphasized here by the way the 'best of men' fail (verses 40–41, 43, 45, 56). Jesus knew the weakness of men, better than they themselves did (verse 31)! He alone could face, with full knowledge of all that it would entail, the fiery trial.

Finally, note the tenderness of Jesus on the way to the cross. The fact that Jesus was acting for others is plainly set out in this passage, and we have already noticed this. But notice that Jesus accompanies his prediction of failure by a prediction of the disciples' welcome after failure (verse 32). Though they fail them he will always welcome them!

Questions

1. If Jesus has forgiven you, can it be truly said that you have forgiven yourself your failures? If not, how can you do so?
2. How do you respond to the Muslims' charge that Jesus cannot be the Son of God because he experienced such agony in the face of death?
3. How can one death save others from death? Is this only symbolic, or in some way real?

Matthew 26:57–75

Who is Jesus?

Matthew describes Jesus' trial before the Sanhedrin to emphasize the claims that Jesus made about himself, and to compare Jesus' boldness with Peter's threefold denial.

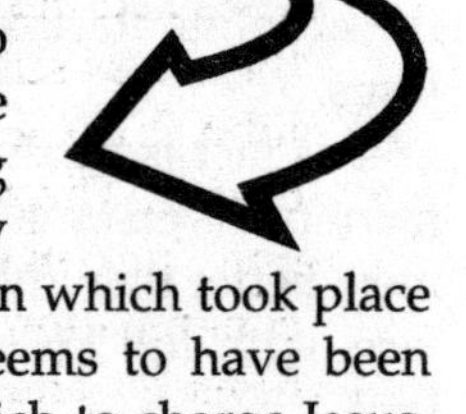

After Jesus' arrest, he was first taken to Annas (John 18:12–14, 19–23) before appearing before Caiaphas. This meeting either preceded, or was the preliminary hearing for, the full meeting of the Sanhedrin which took place early the following morning (27:1–2). It seems to have been intended to establish the grounds upon which to charge Jesus. The great question which occupies these verses is, 'Who is Jesus?' Here before the supreme religious authorities of Israel Jesus provides the answer.

- *Jesus is the Messiah* (the Christ) (verses 63–64). The promised deliverer of God's people had been predicted time and again in the Old Testament; the Jews were anxiously awaiting him, and Jesus claimed to be the deliverer they were expecting. Yet, as the chapter has already indicated, Jesus came to deliver men and women from the guilt and the penalty of sin. The Jews had lost sight of this.

- *Jesus is the Son of God.* 2 Samuel 7:14 and Psalm 2:7 had introduced the idea that the Messiah would be the 'Son of God'. The Jews would not necessarily have understood this to be a reference to deity although Jesus' teaching had already paved the way for this truth (Matthew 21:37). Perhaps it was such apparent claims of Jesus that Caiaphas tried to clarify. Jesus' answer acknowledged it to be so, as does the rest of the New Testament. Jesus truly is 'Immanuel', God with us.

- *Jesus also claimed to be the Son of Man* (verse 64). Jesus qualified the Jews' understanding of messiahship with this phrase. Consistently, in his ministry, the words 'the Son of Man' point to his humiliation (and yet, paradoxically, his authority). He had not come to be some mighty conqueror, but to display his authority in suffering and death. In verse 64 Jesus quotes Psalm 110:4 and Daniel 7:13, which fill out his meaning.

- *Jesus is the builder of the new temple* (verse 61). Though the Jews had misunderstood Jesus' claims, it seems likely that there was substance to the claims made against Jesus (see John 2:19). He made no attempt to refute them (verses 62–63). The temple he would build after three days was one 'not made with hands' (Mark 14:58); but a new congregation centred not upon a building but upon Jesus himself. Thus Jesus declared that the whole of the Old Testament pointed forward to him and found its fulfilment in him and his people.

- *Jesus is enthroned at the place of highest authority* (verse 64). This is the point of the imagery drawn from Daniel 7:13 (and compare 24:30, where we saw that the reference in Daniel is not to the second coming, but rather emphasizes the vindication of one brought into the presence of God). From now on, says Jesus, you will witness evidence that I have been vindicated by my Father. Very soon the empty tomb, the growth of the church from Pentecost onwards, the destruction of the temple and the ending of a Jewish state, and the worldwide expansion of the church even amid the fiercest persecution would bear testimony to the truth of Jesus' claim.

How are men and women to respond?

Rejection is the first response described here. These verses describe not a court of law but a conspiracy to murder. Yet the murder is excused by men pretending to be weighing and assessing the available evidence. They have no intention of discovering the truth, only of lynching Jesus. Sin hates the light, and sinners hate Jesus and will ignore the facts rather than have to bow the knee to him. Yet, at the same time, they will seek to rationalize their unbelief.

The other response described here is betrayal. Jesus was betrayed by all his disciples, not just Judas. Not least, he was betrayed by Peter (verses 69–75). Even those who know the truth can and do betray him. Like Peter they are not prepared for trial (see also verse 41), and can go so far as to curse him. (In verse 74, the NIV has interpreted the text. It could mean *either* that Peter called down curses on himself *or* that he cursed Jesus, though the latter is not unlikely.) But what comfort is implied in these verses! The Peter who cursed his Lord repented with a true repentance (verse 75 and compare 2 Corinthians 7:10). Thus he found the words in Matthew 10:33 to be revoked in his own case. No-one who shows true repentance need ever fear that Jesus will not welcome him or her back. Even if we have blasphemed the name of Jesus, even if we have cursed him, he is ready to accept our repentance and reinstate us.

Questions

1. The Jewish authorities chose to ignore the evidence and pursue their prejudiced plans. How can we be sure that we are not blinded by prejudice?

2. How far should we respect and obey the decisions of our church/denomination/fellowship? Where do we draw the line between healthy discipline and freedom?
3. What examples can you think of which illustrate the various responses which people make to the claims of Jesus? What do you think are their motives in each case?

Matthew 27:1–26

Facing the challenge

The death of Judas and Jesus' trial before Pilate. Matthew illustrates the different reactions men and women had to Jesus.

Some men and women are implacably opposed to Jesus. The Jewish leaders will not stop short of crucifying Jesus even though both the governor and his wife are aware that Jesus is innocent of the charges brought against him (verses 19, 24). It was envious hatred of Jesus which drove these men on (verse 18).

For others, the cost of recognizing Jesus is too high. Pilate illustrates this very well. He could see through the hatred of the religious leaders (verse 18) although, probably, he could see no further. Nevertheless, he prevented himself from coming to a full understanding of Jesus because of his selfish ambitions. What we know about Pilate from elsewhere suggests that he was a proud, cruel and hard man. He eventually turned the whole of the Jewish race against him and, since it is impossible to rule over such opposition, he was recalled to Rome. We see here the beginnings of the pit he dug for himself. Pilate had antagonized the people, and they were ready to question his patriotism (John 19:12). Thus, though he hated the Jews and had no wish to favour them, he was forced to bow to blackmail.

Some men and women prove very fickle in their discipleship. This was true of the crowd (see especially verses 20–25). Only a few days previously they had welcomed Jesus and fêted him like a returning victor (21:1–11). Now they demand his death. Hendriksen, in his commentary *The Gospel of Matthew*, says at this point, 'When the prophet of Galilee was still healing the sick, raising the dead, cleansing the lepers, holding multitudes spellbound by means of his marvellous discourses, he was popular. When he rode into Jerusalem, he was applauded. But now that he is seemingly helpless, and the leaders have used their strongest arguments to persuade the people to demand his crucifixion, they turn their backs on him.'

But why such a turn against Jesus? So long as Jesus held out to them the prospect of meeting those needs or wants which they believed to be important, they would stand by him; but not a moment longer. When he 'failed', he would experience the whiplash of their emotions.

Other people have a superstitious reverence for Jesus, something apparently true of Pilate's wife (verse 9). Her dream had been unsettling. Under its influence she took certain steps to secure Jesus' (or was it her husband's?) safety. What subsequently happened we do not know. However, it is most likely that when the effects of the dream wore off, so did her concern.

Finally, some people manifest a sorrow for sin which falls short of true repentance. This was true of Judas (verses 3–10). He was filled with remorse but unrepentant. He regretted his action and was smitten by his conscience. Tears may have flowed but, at heart, he was not sorry for what he had done to Jesus: only sorry that he had let himself down.

Questions

1. To what extent is your faith one which trusts Jesus for more than simply supplying your needs? What more should be involved?
2. Are there those in your church who appear to be 'fair

weather' Christians? What can be done to help them to true faith? Can it grow naturally and gradually, or do they need to be confronted with the inadequacy of their beliefs?

3. Corruption of legal processes is a worldwide phenomenon today. What does Jesus' experience call us to say or do about such corruption?

The trial of Jesus

It is not always easy to harmonize what Matthew records with the other accounts of Jesus' trial and death. Nor is it always easy to account for the events as described in the gospels when they are compared with other non-biblical sources. The scholarly commentaries debate these issues, and some conclude that the various accounts are so hopelessly muddled that harmonization is impossible. Such a judgment must only ever be reached as a last resort. The fact is that the gospel-writers lived a lot nearer the events they describe than we do, and premature judgments of their accuracy are, therefore, out of place. In view of the accuracy of the Bible-writers on all those issues which can be tested, we have no reason to doubt their testimony concerning Jesus' trial and death.

Matthew 27:27–56

Jesus' death

Matthew's account of the crucifixion highlights the mockery that Jesus received from Gentile soldiers, Jewish passers-by, the religious leaders of Judaism and even criminals.

Jesus was despised and rejected. We have identified the various groups who mocked Jesus; they represent all sorts of people. Moreover, Jesus was mocked for both his claims and his actions (verse 43, especially). Granted, the claims had been amazing: to be Israel's king (verses 29, 37), the builder of the new temple (verse 40), the Son of God (verse 43). But his mighty works ought to have alerted people to the need to examine those claims more fully. However, this was true neither then nor now.

One phrase here ascribes to Jesus the highest possible dignity. It is 'the Son of God' (verses 43, 54). Though the centurion may not have understood the full meaning of the phrase, it is clear that Matthew and the other New Testament writers intended us to know that Jesus fully shared the same divine nature as the Father: He was 'very God of very God', God become man, 'Immanuel, God with us'.

Thus, Christianity builds its foundations on the highest ground: the revelation of God to men in his incarnate Son. This makes it altogether unique and exclusive. Four great truths about Jesus' work are taught here.

- *Jesus refused to save himself so that he could save others* (verse 42). There was a real truth in the mockery of his scorners. Jesus had rendered himself powerless to do anything to alleviate his suffering in order that he might avert the suffering of others.

- *Jesus suffered for sin* (verses 45–46). These two verses emphasize that it was the penalty for sin which Jesus bore. Darkness in the Bible is the usual symbol of judgment for sin, and so here the darkness indicated in a visible and symbolic form the fact that Jesus was being made 'a sin for us'. But this is not all, since verse 46 teaches an inexplicable truth, that temporarily the threefold unity of God was broken. We cannot understand this mystery. But we can comprehend the lesson it teaches. For surely it declares both the seriousness of sin and the divine love for sinners which could bring such hurt to Father and Son that we might go free!
- *Jesus has purchased forgiveness and access to God for all his followers* (verse 51). The veil in the temple symbolized the unapproachableness of God as a consequence of man's sin. Only a preceding sacrifice for sin could enable the High Priest to enter: and then only once a year (compare Leviticus 16). But the tearing of the veil speaks of a free access grounded upon a final, unrepeatable sacrifice.
- *Jesus' death has brought the curse to an end* (verses 52, 53). In this strange story we are reminded that death is the penalty for sin but, where sin has been finally dealt with, death is brought to an end. It is true that we still die. But Jesus is the firstfruits (1 Corinthians 15:20) of the dead. His death guarantees our final resurrection and the creation of a new heaven and a new earth.

Questions

1. Imagine yourself standing where the centurion stood. What do you see? What conclusions do you reach from what you see? Some preachers and evangelists speak in detail about the physical agonies of crucifixion. Do you think this is right?
2. The crucifixion of Jesus has been painted and portrayed in art in many ways over the centuries. In what ways could such pictures be helpful – or unhelpful – in grasping the meaning of the cross for ourselves?

3. What truths do you believe are central to the Christian message? How would you sum it up briefly for an enquirer?

Matthew 27:57 – 28:15

Facing the evidence

Some of the evidence for the resurrection is offered by Matthew, with a reminder of the folly of unbelief.

These verses (with 28:16–20) comprise the final section of Matthew's gospel. Five paragraphs are carefully balanced:

27:57–61 Jesus dead and buried.
27:62–66 Setting the guard.
28:1–10 The empty tomb and the risen Lord.
28:11–15 Report of the guard.
28:16–20 Jesus alive and sovereign.

This structure clearly emphasizes that Jesus is risen in order to rule. In particular, the first four paragraphs (which are under consideration here) emphasize both the fact of the empty tomb and the resurrection appearances of Jesus. The last paragraph emphasizes Jesus' reconciliation with the disciples and their (and our) great commission.

Matthew stresses the overwhelmingly strong evidence for the resurrection. This is demonstrated in a number of ways.

- The people who actually witnessed the burial of Jesus in Joseph of Arimathea's tomb (27:61) were the first witnesses of the empty tomb (28:6). There could, therefore, be little doubt that they went to the right place.

- The religious authorities of the day could not deny the fact of the empty tomb, despite all attempts to ensure the predicted event would not happen (28:11–15). After all, the very men who had kept the dead Jesus a prisoner were those who bore testimony to the fact that the body was gone.
- The presence of the guard at the tomb and the fact that the priests thought up the excuse of grave-stealing is testimony to the falsehood of the suggestion that the tomb was robbed. Moreover, it is absurd. Would all the guards sleep? And if they all slept, how did they *know* that the disciples stole the body.
- It is not possible to argue that Jesus was not really dead and that, in the cool of the tomb, he revived and came out. Such an 'apparition' might have explained the soldiers' senselessness, but how could Jesus move the stone and break the seal (verses 60, 66)?

Jesus is alive!

But this passage does not merely speak of the empty tomb. It bears witness to the bodily appearance of Jesus (verses 8–10). It was not merely the empty tomb that convinced Jesus' followers, it was the fact that they actually met him: no ghostly apparition, but the bodily Jesus whose feet could be grasped.

With the evidence of Matthew's gospel alone we can see the strength of the testimony to the reality of the resurrection. Dead men don't come back to life: but this one apparently did!

This passage also demonstrates the folly of unbelief. Despite the overwhelmingly strong evidence, men and women (both then and now) do not believe in the resurrection of Jesus. Some have never given any considered thought to the matter. But for the overwhelming majority, there is another reason for disbelief: they don't *want* to believe it. Even faced with the evidence of the empty tomb that Jesus had predicted, and for which they could offer no explanation, people then would not believe. Men and women have an amazing capacity to refuse to believe what they don't want to.

The religious leaders of Jesus' day were such people. They had no interest in the truth (Jesus' trial had shown that), so even the overwhelming evidence before their very eyes could not move them. Their response was to fabricate a story to explain away the evidence; a story altogether more unbelievable than the truth. And men and women are often no different today. They simply will not face the truth fair and square 'like men!' Accusing Christians (like their Master before them) of fraudulence (27:64), they are guilty of the very failing that they see in others.

Why does this happen? The religious leaders of the day would not accept Jesus because of their pride. As with all men and women, they were selfish by nature. To recognize Jesus for who he was and is would force them to acknowledge that there was one who had a supreme claim to their lives. And for the descendants of the first couple who had wanted to be as God, this was and is too much.

Questions

1. What reasons can you offer for the truth of the resurrection?
2. Why do even religious people today sometimes say belief in the resurrection is not necessary? What is left of Christianity if the resurrection has not happened?
3. Myths and fairy-stories are full of gods and men and women who die and come to life again. What is the difference between them and this story of Jesus' resurrection?

Matthew 28:16–20

Into all the world!

This is the triumphant conclusion of Matthew's gospel. It prepares the way for the 'greater things' that Jesus will accomplish through his people in the ages to follow.

The concluding words of Matthew's gospel stress the relevance of Jesus' words (and all that has been previously described) to everyone who is a Christian. Jesus addressed the Eleven (verse 16), but his words are clearly given to them as representatives of all those who will follow in their footsteps 'to the very end of the age' (verse 20). It is not even to leaders, therefore, that these words are primarily addressed, but to every congregation of God's people and to every individual in those congregations. His command is one which none of us who claim to be Christians can honestly avoid.

The only command in these verses is 'make disciples' (verse 19). That is the responsibility that, in one way or another, rests on us all. But, we might reasonably ask, what is a 'disciple', and how can we make one? Jesus explains by giving a threefold answer.

- *We make disciples by going*. This is not really a command. It describes, rather, the first of three steps to making a disciple. We are to go – 'to all sorts and conditions of men'. We are to determine where we should go according to the assessment of the gifts which God has given us. But whether we are called to our neighbours or workmates or to the other end of the world, we all share a missionary 'call', for a missionary is not a special Christian who witnesses to Jesus overseas. We are all missionaries – wherever we are placed by the Lord.

- *We are to baptize.* Baptism is the response of faith, the sign and seal of conversion. So the church is assured that there will be converts, and that those converts are to be visibly identified with the people of God.
- *We are to teach all that Jesus taught us to obey.* We do not teach abstract truths, but truths which transform lives and which have already transformed ours. Thus, we are to disciple others by showing as well as by speaking. There is nothing more powerful in evangelism than lives which confirm the truth of the message.

So, as individuals and as a church, we are to work out how best we can reach others with the gospel. Then we are to take up our responsibility as missionaries. Jesus gives the reason for such a calling, and offers assurances to those engaged in such missionary service. The reason we are to go to everyone is that Jesus is now Lord over all (verse 18). We have a right and a responsibility to declare to them all their duties to him.

But Jesus knows what we are like. Thus, he adds two assurances. First, he offers the guarantee of his power. We cannot know the precise reason for the doubts of some of the disciples (verse 17). Perhaps it doesn't matter for, more importantly, it teaches us that the early disciples were weak, tremulous people – just like us. To such people (as to us) there is great comfort in knowing that we do not go in our strength: indeed we could achieve no good if we did. We have no resources but those of one who has all power and that is sufficient. We expect so little as believers because we doubt the Lord's words. And though he does not assure us of constant success, he does encourage us to expect fruit from our labour (even if it is sometimes long delayed).

Secondly, Jesus offers the guarantee of his presence (verse 20). This verse is often used as a basis for 'cosy reassurance', but it is not that. Rather, it is the basis for our mission; and what a wonderful basis it is. It is not simply that we are left to our own devices with the power that he has granted, but that he himself comes along with us. Whenever we go out, we always go with a minimum of two of us! In the hardship and trial as well as in the joy and success, he is there by our side. What comfort there is in the assurance that he comes even into the darkest place with us!

Questions

1. What 'missions' must I undertake on my own (nevertheless with Jesus)? What 'missions' must be attempted in twos or in larger groups? What can we learn from the answers?
2. It has been said that churches exist for the benefit of non-members. How far is this really true of your fellowship?
3. If the church is to go into all the world, why is it that most missionary activity is concentrated in Africa and Asia? What other 'fields' need help, perhaps nearer home?

Further reading

R. T. France, 'Matthew', in *New Bible Commentary, 21st Century edition* (IVP, 1994).

R. T. France, *Matthew,* Tyndale New Testament Commentary (IVP, 1989).

J. R. W. Stott, *The Message of the Sermon on the Mount,* Bible Speaks Today (IVP, 1978).

J. C. Ryle, *Matthew,* Crossway Classic Commentary, series editors Alister McGrath and J. I. Packer (Crossway Books, 1993). A nineteenth-century classic brought up to date.

William Barclay, *Gospel of Matthew,* 2 volumes (The Saint Andrew Press, 1975). Excellent for background.

D. A. Carson, *Matthew,* Expositors' Bible Commentary (Zondervan, 1984). A more advanced commentary, with an excellent defence of the historical accuracy of the gospel with lines of application.

Questions

Further reading